Also by Lewis Grizzard:

WHEN MY LOVE RETURNS FROM THE LADIES ROOM, WILL I BE TOO OLD TO CARE?*

MY DADDY WAS A PISTOL AND I'M A SON OF A GUN

SHOOT LOW, BOYS—THEY'RE RIDIN' SHETLAND PONIES*

ELVIS IS DEAD AND I DON'T FEEL SO GOOD MYSELF

IF LOVE WERE OIL, I'D BE ABOUT A QUART LOW

THEY TORE OUT MY HEART AND STOMPED THAT SUCKER FLAT

DON'T SIT UNDER THE GRITS TREE WITH ANYONE ELSE BUT ME

WON'T YOU COME HOME, BILLY BOB BAILEY?

KATHY SUE LOUDERMILK, I LOVE YOU

Comedy Albums

ON THE ROAD WITH LEWIS GRIZZARD

LEWIS GRIZZARD LIVE

LET'S HAVE A PARTY WITH LEWIS GRIZZARD

*Published by Ballantine Books

Don't Bend Over In The Garden, Granny, You Know Them Taters Got Eyes

Lewis Grizzard

BALLANTINE BOOKS • NEW YORK

Grateful acknowledgment is made to the following for permission to reprint previously published material:
SBK APRIL MUSIC INC.: Excerpts from the lyrics to "Eat Me Alive" by Glen Tipton, Robert Halford, and Kenneth K. Downing. Copyright © 1984 SBK April Music Inc./Crewglen Ltd./Ebonytree Ltd./Geargate Ltd. All rights controlled and administered by SBK April Music Inc. All rights reserved. International copyright secured. Used by permission.

TREE PUBLISHING CO., INC.: Excerpts from the lyrics to "Thirty-nine and Holding" by Ed Bruce and Ron Peterson. Copyright © 1980 Tree Publishing Co., Inc. All rights reserved. International Copyright secured. Used by permission of the publisher.

Library of Congress Catalog Card Number: 88-40171

ISBN 0-345-36094-x

This edition published by arrangement with Villard Books, a division of Random House, Inc.

Manufactured in the United States of America

First Ballantine Books Edition: October 1989

EVEN I'M SMART ENOUGH TO KNOW
YOU DON'T GO DEDICATING
A BOOK ABOUT SEX TO ANYBODY.

Don't Bend Over In The Garden, Granny, You Know Them Taters Got Eyes

CHAPTER ONE

I decided to write a book about sex and its awesome effect on our lives for a number of reasons. I shall list them:

1. Dr. Ruth talks funny and I can't make out what she's saying half the time. Dr. Ruth looks like a very nice person and she probably knows her sex as well as anybody else, but with her accent, there is a danger somebody might misunderstand something she said and become injured—or, at the best, terribly embarrassed—trying to follow her instructions.

Let's say Dr. Ruth was jabbering about as she does and says, "Never have sex without a condom."

With her accent it might come out, "Never have sex with a quorum." This, of course, could lead to a sudden increase in group sex and when you get a lot of people together like that, somebody could get hurt, even if it's only their feelings.

The closest I ever got to group sex was the time Loot Starkins brought two of his sows over to my uncle's farm to have them bred with my uncle's prize boar, Big Jake. You get four or five thousand pounds of pork in the heat of passion and you have some sort of action going on. I suppose, although I didn't know it at the time, what I was watching was a *ménage da hog*.

I have done a lot of thinking about group sex, however, and I can deal with three participants in relation to who does what to whom. Get me over three, however, and I'm terribly confused. Throw five together, for instance, and somebody obviously has to be left out and that's where some feelings are going to get hurt.

My book will be clear, concise and in plain English, in order to take up any slack left by Dr. Ruth. More on specific wordage later.

2. Sex, it now has been proven, will kill you. We need a book on how to have sex without getting killed. If AIDS were not enough of a worry, I read in an aviation newsletter where a guy was flying a light plane out

west and it crashed, killing him and his female companion.

A Federal Aviation Administration report said that due to certain injuries found on the pilot and the position of his female companion, the couple very likely was engaged in an act of oral sex at the time of the crash. Somebody needs to write a book about sex and mention that it has no place in the cockpit, something I don't think Dr. Ruth nor Masters and Johnson has mentioned.

A story has it that several years ago Gloria Steinem, the women's rights activist, boarded a commercial flight and heard the following announcement: "Ladies and gentlemen, this is an historic moment in commercial aviation history. For the first time, a woman pilot will be in complete charge of your flight."

Ms. Steinem was, quite naturally, impressed, and asked a flight attendant, "May I go up to the cockpit and congratulate the woman pilot?"

"Sure," said the attendant, "only we don't call it a 'cockpit' anymore."

This book will, incidentally, offer an occasional joke or story with sexual overtones. There are a lot of reasons for that, too. Mainly, it's because most people find jokes with sexual overtones amusing . . . that and the fact that 98 percent of the jokes I've ever heard had sexual overtones.

In other words, jokes without sexual overtones are hard to find, and most of them aren't funny.

Example: What do you call a boomerang that won't come back? A stick.

3. I was considering ideas for books and somebody suggested I do one on sex.

"You don't need to write something that is filthy," I was told. "Just get in there and point out how sex makes the world go around and how much a part of everybody's life it is and how we're always talking about it and laughing about it and getting totally confused by it."

"But," I pointed out, "there have already been tons of books about sex."

"Yes," my counsel continued, "but all those books were by alleged experts on the subject. Are you an expert on sex?"

"Of course not," I said, "I wasn't in the army and I missed all those training films."

"Then that's the angle you take. You're just as dumbfounded and lost about sex as most of the rest of the population. Your book can make others who are confused feel like they are not alone out there in the great sexual cosmos. Think of yourself as a public service announcement."

"Like a message from the National Health Institute about condoms?"

"That's it. You're one of those, a brief pause in next year's literary world that says, 'Listen up, people. We've got to talk about sex here. We've got to have a few laughs about it, we've got to put it in perspective, and we've got to discuss ways to keep from getting killed by it.' Did you see the movie *Fatal Attraction*, incidentally?"

"I did."

"Did you know the rabbit was going to get it?"

"As soon as I saw that rabbit, I knew it was a goner, but I never thought Glenn Close would stoop so low as to boil it alive."

"My point is," my adviser went on, "that sex almost cost Michael Douglas his life, his family, and his career in that movie, and it got the rabbit boiled alive.

"Regardless of how many books have been written about sex, there's always room for another one, especially one that will suggest that if you decide to have an extramarital relationship, you can wind up in a horrible stew."

"I see your point," I said, now needing only a couple more reasons to forge ahead on my book about sex.

4. The year 1987, when I began writing my book, was a banner year for sex, which makes my book topical. Think of all the big stories of '87 that have sexual themes:

Jim and Tammy Faye Bakker and Jessica Hahn, et

al.: They're thinking of making a movie about all that called *The Three Bimbos.*

Gary Hart, Donna Rice, the Monkey Business, *and the* Miami Herald: "Your house or the White House?"

Oral Roberts and His Twin Brother, Anal: I just made that up to show you I do have some creativity when it comes to writing about sex.

Ollie North and Fawn Hall: I don't believe Ollie fooled around with his ace evidence-shredder, but there were more than a few eyebrows lifted when some weeks after Col. North testified in the Iran-contra hearings, Fawn was arrested for eating a banana in a Washington rail station.

You Don't Think There Is Anything Sexy About a Banana? I'll prove it to you. In Carroll County, Georgia, a few miles west of Atlanta, a local health teacher got into big trouble with school officials and parents for using a cucumber to show students the proper way to apply a condom.

"At least," the health instructor said in her defense, "I didn't use a banana."

Vanna White: Showed her vowel movements, not to mention most of everything else, in a *Playboy* pictorial.

Pat Robertson: It was learned that the evangelist-presidential candidate's future wife became pregnant before their marriage, which brings up another one of those jokes with sexual overtones I will toss in from time to time.

A motorist is traveling through Alabama and he stops at a small town for gasoline. As his tank is being filled, he looks on one side of the street and sees the FIRST CHURCH OF THE ENLIGHTENED. He looks on the other side of the street and sees the SECOND CHURCH OF THE ENLIGHTENED.

Confused, he asks the man pumping the gas, "What's the difference between those two churches?"

"Very simple," the man answers. "The First Church of the Enlightened believes Moses' mother found him in the bullrushes. The Second Church of the Enlightened believes, 'Yeah, that's what she says.'"

But it was the fifth reason that ended all my doubts.

5. Sex books historically sell a lot of copies.

Do you think I'm still writing books at the advanced age of forty-two just because I like to type? Of course not. I have a profit motive here.

You remember how hard writing was back in school, don't you? It doesn't come any easier after you're out of school.

I just want to make enough money to send my dog to school so he can learn to read.

You didn't know dogs could go to school and learn to read?

Junior went off to college, and his father was quite proud of him.

First thing Junior does is get into a fraternity poker game and lose all his money. He calls his father.

"Daddy," he says, "you'll never believe what they can do here at the university."

"What's that, son?" his father asks.

"They can teach dogs to read."

"You're kiddin' me."

"Dad, I'm serious. Now, I know how much you love that hound of yours, ol' Blue. Why don't you put him on the train and send him up here to learn to read?"

The father did love ol' Blue and wanted the best for him, as well as for his son.

"How much would it cost?" the father asked.

"A thousand dollars," said the son.

"And you're sure they can teach ol' Blue to read?"

"Absolutely."

"Okay," said the father, "I'll wire you a thousand dollars and send ol' Blue up on the train."

The son gets the thousand and ties ol' Blue with a leash outside the fraternity house. A few more weeks pass, and the boy gets the word from his girlfriend that's she pregnant. He needs some cash in a hurry. He calls his father back.

"*Dad?*" he says.

"*Yeah, son,*" his father replies. "*How's ol' Blue doing in reading class?*"

"*You wouldn't believe it, Dad. Ol' Blue's reading everything in sight—Plato, Burns, history books, even science books.*"

"*That's great, son. When you going to send him back?*"

"*Dad,*" the son went on. "*I've got some more exciting news for you. Now that they've taught ol' Blue to read, they want to teach him to talk.*"

"*They can do that?*"

"*They taught him to read, didn't they? Wouldn't you like to be able to talk to ol' Blue and have him talk back to you?*"

"*That would be nice, son. Ol' Blue could tell me all about what he's read. How much would that cost?*"

"*Just another thousand,*" said the son.

So the father wires another thousand and the son gets out of another jam.

Soon, however, it's Christmas and it's time for the son to return home with ol' Blue. His father calls him.

"*Everybody in town's excited about ol' Blue coming home,*" the father explains. "*We just can't wait to hear him read to us. The mayor's coming out and so's the high school band. We'll see you at the station.*"

The son is, of course, quite perplexed. How will he get out of this?

He boards the train with ol' Blue. During a layover, he leaves the train station and goes and buys a gun. He walks ol' Blue out in the alley and shoots him.

"Sorry, ol' Blue," he says, "but I just don't have a choice."

He arrives home and there's the crowd and the band waiting at the station.

"Son!" his father yells. "Glad to have you home. But where's ol' Blue?"

"Could I have a word in private, Dad?" the son asks.

They step over away from the crowd and the son whispers to his father:

"I've got something to tell you, Dad," he begins. "This morning before I got on the train, I was shaving and ol' Blue was sitting on the john reading The Wall Street Journal.

"All of a sudden, he looks up from the paper and says, 'Does your mother know your ol' man is still messing with that waitress down at the diner?'"

Before he could go any further, the boy's father grabbed him and said, "Son, you did shoot that lyin' son of a bitch, didn't you?"

I'm not the least embarrassed admitting I want this book to sell. This is America, we have a capitalistic society, and I like an occasional bottle of wine with a cork in it.

Sex sells cars, clothes, cigarettes, watches, grain elevators, television programs, magazines, and I wouldn't be surprised if sex weren't somehow involved in the Louisiana Purchase.

So, if sex helps to sell this book, then so be it.

Except for the fact that because the book does have to do with sex, I don't want to exclude some of those who have bought my books before.

I don't want them to think this is just going to be another one of those sleazy things with a lot of nasty language and nasty situations. I promise I will not use a single really dirty word in this book.

I might use a "hell" or a "damn" here and there and I've already used "son of a bitch," but they use these words on prime time television, and have for years.

Remember that my mother is still alive, and I would never embarrass her by saying things like Eddie Murphy and Richard Pryor say. Also, there's my minister, several of my ex-teachers, and my former Little League baseball coach to consider.

I don't want any of them reading this book and then saying, "He wasn't raised that way."

You might ask at this point, however, "How are you going to write about sex and not be specific about certain body parts and functions?"

I've got that covered, and it all came to me when I

was a guest of Alan Colmes's call-in radio talk show on station WNBC in New York.

You know how many weird people there are in New York and how many of them dearly would enjoy calling a talk radio station and saying a lot of dirty words.

As a means of dealing with all this, Alan Colmes came up with a great idea: He asked his listeners to offer new dirty words to replace old dirty words. Callers could say all the new dirty words they wanted to on the air and mean the same thing they would have if they had been using the old dirty words. The difference would be that Mr. Colmes would be able to keep his job and WNBC would be able to keep its license.

After several weeks, Alan developed his list of alternative dirty words. I obtained a copy of the list and offer it here. I am not about to tell you which new word replaces which old word. That would take the fun out of it. Decide for yourself what stands for what:

—Fatza Macher

—Yippus

—Fuzba

—Hobbledy Goo (female)

—Hobbledy Gee (male)

—Pogue

—Wamp

—Fleen spunt

—Gooba dust

—Schmeck

—Gerka

—Clivea

—Boink

After reading these words, there is the delicious desire to make up sentences using some of them. Here's mine:

Marvin walked into the bar and saw Hilda brooding over a whiskey sour. Her skirt was cut all the way to her wamp and her gerkas seemed about to go public at any moment.

"You know, Hilda," Marvin began as he reached the bar. "I'll bet you have a lovely fuzba."

"You fatza macher," said Hilda, looking up from her drink. "Why don't you go pogue yourself."

"You're going to regret this, you fleen spunt," said Marvin.

"Schmeck," said Hilda.

Marvin went home and turned on the Playboy Channel and watched the last moments of the movie, Deep

17

Clivea. *Unfortunately, the gooba dust scenes had all been cut.*

After reviewing what I just wrote, however, I realized these terms were so suggestive, I probably shouldn't use them in my book either, or I would be just another one of those people who write sex books with all those terms that, although not on anybody's *verboten* list, still aren't suitable for a book with such a high-toned purpose as this one.

I first came across words and terms like that when I was nine and my boyhood friend and idol, Weyman C. Wannamaker, Jr., a great American, allowed me to read a copy of a sex novel entitled *Suburban Interlude*, which he found in his father's socks drawer.

I took the book and went underneath my grandfather's scuppernong vines, where there was total privacy, with the exception of the fruit flies, and read it.

I came across a great many of these literary sexual terms in sentences like, "Marvin thrust his turgid member into Hilda's love canal."

I promise not to write sentences like that, or use any of the following phrases and terms:

—Love muscle

—Heat-seeking missile

—Heaving orbs

—Tunnel of lust

—Crescendo of waves breaking through her taut body

—Her oohs turned to ahs

—As his rough, calloused hands reached the pink softness of her . . .

—Dampness

—Throbbing

—Rhythmic

—Pulsating

—Milky

—Or, ". . . and they were one"

Yet that still doesn't answer the question: "Okay, so you aren't going to use any of that. What are you going to use?"

(Why did I hear my fourth grade teacher's voice when I typed those words?)

What I am going to do is use everyday, happy little words we all use from time to time when it is not appropriate to use the *real* words, as when you tell a joke in front of your parents-in-law that they might think is funny, but would be shocked if you didn't change a few things here and there.

Let's take the act of sexual intercourse. I can't come out and say what Richard Pryor or Eddie Murphy would say, and since I don't want to sound overly technical, I think I'll use the following:

1. Went to bed. We discussed that earlier.
2. Had sex. You read that in the daily papers.
3. Did it.

I think "did it" or "do it" or "does it" probably will be the most frequent term I use, in this instance. It was what we said when I was growing up. As in, "Did you hear who did it?", "Shirley won't let me do it," or, "I hear Cassandra does it on the first date."

And what about female breasts? Any book about sex will have to deal with them. Why don't I use PG-13 terms like "bongos," "knockers," "headlamps," and "biggest ones in three counties"?

As for the female hindparts, I suggest "la boomba," "seatcover," or "rascadango."

The major problem, however, will be what to call the key organs involved here. For the female, I have thought of referring to her "woo-woo." For the male, I have considered using the term "mule."

But I don't like either one of those. What I decided upon was using the term "business" to refer to both. "Business" is a harmless word, yet it gets the job done. Let's try "business" out in a joke:

Big John was a fine specimen of a man, and every lady in the neighborhood could hardly take her eyes off him when he strode down the street.

One day, Charlene, who was a bit of a rounder, drank her beer out of the bottle, shot pool for money, and ate raw wienies, couldn't stand it any longer. So when Big John came walking into the pool hall, she confronted him.

"Big John," she asked, "how big is your neck?"

"Twenty-six inches," he replied.

"How do you know that?" she asked again.

"What's wrong with you?" said Big John. "I take a tape measure and put it around my neck and it says twenty-six inches."

"How big is your chest?"

"Forty-eight inches."

"How do you measure that?"

"Just like my neck, woman. I put a tape measure around my chest and it says forty-eight inches."

"How small is your waist?"

"Thirty inches."

"A big man like you with a small waist like that. You're really built, Big John, but how do you measure your waist?"

"I ain't got time for much more of this," said Big John. "I measure my waist like I measure my neck and chest. I put a tape measure around it and it says thirty inches."

"Big John," Charlene wanted to know. "How big is your business?"

21

"Why are you asking about my business?" said Big John. "You leave my business out of this."

"I just want to know how big a business a man like you has."

"Six inches," said Big John.

"Six inches?" replied Charlene, in disbelief. "You mean you've got that big ol' neck and that big ol' chest and that little ol' bitty waist and all you got in the way of business is six inches?"

"That's right," said Big John.

"Well," said Charlene, "how do you measure that?" Big John smiled. "From the floor."

The only questions that remain, I suppose, are:
1. What areas of sex will the book involve?

Since this is merely the first chapter, I'm still not certain. However, some of the areas I hope to cover are honeymoons, German sex shops (and other stories with an international flavor), a stripper named Fonda Love, buying condoms, something called the Panty of the Month Club, Richard Nixon (You don't believe there's a sexual angle there? Trust me.), gay people floating down a river with no clothes on in broad daylight, sex in sports, sex in the cinema, sex on television, with mentions of such things as feminine hygiene products, oysters, the dictionary, George Washington, bowling, and those letters people allegedly write in to *Penthouse* magazine.

2. Should young people read this book?

Certainly. Many parents, of course, are against their children learning about sex. These people are idiots, not to mention doo-doo pots. The real reason most probably want to keep their children in the dark about sex is they don't know anything about it either, and they are afraid they will have to ask their children if a question comes up about girl-on-top or crotchless leather underpants.

Don't worry, kids. If your parents don't want you to know anything about sex, ask them for a few bucks to go to the mall and play video games and then spend the money on this book.

Sorry there aren't any pictures, but there should be enough information in these pages to make you aware of at least one of the primary truths about sex: There's nothing inherently dirty about sex, but if you try real hard and use your imagination you can overcome that quite easily.

A better way to explain that is to tell you of a friend of mine who met a young lady and after several days (this was back during the Spanish-American War) they had sex.

After it was over the lady turned to my friend and asked, "Do you think we've sinned?"

To which my friend replied, "I don't know about you, but I did all I could do."

One final note: This book will not attempt to condone

nor vilify any sexual activity. If it's no bother to you and gives joy to others, then do as you wish.

And 3., What about oral and anal? Well, Oral's still out there in Tulsa begging for money, and his twin brother Anal is a well-respected faith-healing proctologist in Skokie, Illinois.

CHAPTER TWO

Thre are a lot of people who have never had sex. That's a stupid statement. Of course, there are. What I mean here is there are a lot of people we presume have had sex, but, it is my belief, they never have. We ought to get these people out of the way before we go any further.

I figure Richard Nixon has never had sex. I know he has children, but I think they were adopted, or fathered by Pat Boone as a favor, as I simply cannot picture Richard Nixon having sex.

For one thing, I'm convinced he was born in a dull, blue suit and has slept in one the rest of his life. I suppose you can sleep in a suit and still have sex, but

I don't think Richard Nixon would even try it because he might get something on his tie, and Nixon strikes me as somebody who would absolutely hate to get something on his tie.

You've met people like that before. They're stuffy and fastidious and wear wing-tip shoes and you'd like to see them try to eat barbecued chicken without getting one speck of sauce somewhere on their persons.

Not only can I not picture Richard Nixon having sex, I can't picture anybody having sex with him, not even his wife, Pat, who probably feigned enough headaches during her married life that she could be the Advil poster child.

In order to have sex, you've got to have at least a little something cool or suave about you, and you've got to let your hair (as well as your pants) down at least a little.

I can't picture Nixon doing that. He might have sex if he could do it by mail, but that's about it.

The only reason we might believe that Nixon ever had sex is that when he said, "You won't have Dick Nixon to kick around anymore," he might have meant his S&M thing was in the past.

But I doubt Nixon was ever into whips and chains, except for the time G. Gordon Liddy came over to the Oval Office and asked Nixon to beat him up with a rubber hose so he could show the president his loyalty.

"Go fry yourself a rat, Gordon," the president probably said. "When I need some dirty work done, you'll be the first one I call."

That brings up Henry Kissinger, Nixon's secretary of state. I know that Henry was once hailed as Washington's most eligible bachelor before he married what's-her-name who's so thin and tall and thumps cigarette ashes on the floor of the White House at cocktail receptions (I was at a White House dinner once and saw her do it),* but I can't picture Henry Kissinger having sex, either.

And even if he did, I bet he never took off his glasses, and then spent thirty minutes analyzing the entire procedure and came to the ultimate conclusion, "Ve dum de doom ve dum de doom," which is how Henry Kissinger says, "This is a lot more fun than talking to the president about how he always wanted to be a sportswriter."

I don't think evangelist Jerry Falwell ever has had sex before, either, which some may feel difficult to believe what with the history of evangelism and its recent episodes of fooling around in the wrong pew. (See Bakker, Jim.)

I can see Elmer Gantry doing it every chance he got. In fact, I did see the movie *Elmer Gantry,* and I thought Burt Lancaster did a splendid job of portraying the

*Do it, as in thump ashes—not "do it."

Brother Gantry who had the hell hots for everything that wore a skirt and didn't sing bass. But not Jerry Falwell.

He looks too much like a frog to have had sex. The next time you see Jerry Falwell, notice how toadlike he looks. He looks like he could fling out his tongue and pick off an unassuming fly at twenty feet. He probably sits in his office and does that at night after counting his money.

Jerry Falwell seems to be the kind of person who, if he could, would get rid of sex forever. When he talks about sex, he uses the term "fornicating."

The only people who say "fornicating" are people who spit on you when they talk and started branding people with scarlet letters when witch hunts went out of style.

The next time you hear Jerry Falwell talking about the evils of sex, watch how his eyes get wild and his lower lip trembles when he spits out the word "fornicate!"—which he always says with an exclamation point on the end. Examples:

"Jim Bakker *fornicated!*"

"They are *fornicating* on the campuses of this country!"

"The *fornicators* are in control of the media!"

"Kill the *fornicators!*"

Even back in biology class in 1962 when the teacher discussed the reproduction of the salamander (they weren't allowed to go any further than that), he didn't use the term "fornicate." He stuck to "fertilizes" and "mates with." Later, the biology teacher was caught fertilizing one of the substitute teachers over behind where he kept dead salamanders in jars of formaldehyde. He was kicked out of the school system and last we heard was out west somewhere trying to figure out just how turtles do it with that shell and all.

There was a rumor Jerry Falwell had once engaged in oral sex. That turned out not to be the case, however. All he did was stand in one corner of the room and trade "fornicate-you's" with Jim Bakker when they were trying to decide who was in charge of the PTL Club.

Here are some other people who I'm not sure ever have had sex and the reasons why:

PORTER WAGONER: By the time he gets all those rhinestones off, the feeling has passed.

XAVIERA HOLLANDER: All that's probably just a lot of talk.

DR. RUTH: Ditto, plus she's too short.

YASSIR ARAFAT: Too ugly.

WILBUR ON *MR. ED:* Ed had too much pride.

BROOKE SHIELDS: Her mother hasn't told her about it yet.

MARCEL MARCEAU:

DORIS DAY: Actually, she had sex before, but she gave it up when she became a virgin. (With apologies to Oscar Levant who once said, "I knew Doris Day before she became a virgin.")

CONAN THE BARBARIAN: He wanted to have sex, but his shield and sword kept getting in the way.

PRINCE CHARLES: Much too proper to deal with anything so common. Sent in his sperm to Princess Di from his polo matches by Royal Courier.

BOY GEORGE: Neither sex will have him.

ROY ROGERS: The King of the Cowboys, my childhood hero, didn't have time for such frivolity what with things so rough out on the range, which also could mean Dale and Smiley Burnette were more than just friends.

HERSCHEL WALKER: Has always been shy around girls and there aren't any fast enough to catch him.

NAPOLEON BONAPARTE: Ever notice in his pictures his pants didn't have a fly?

WALLY AND THE BEAV: America wouldn't have stood for it.

MATT DILLON: God knows he had his chances after Miss Kitty closed the Longbranch, but that's the sort of stand-up, no-nonsense guy he was. The jury is still out on Festus, however.

ANDY GRIFFITH AND HELEN CRUMP: Want to go over to Mt. Pilot and eat Chinese?

SUPERMAN: Little-known fact he was impotent. That's what X-ray eyes will do for you.

IVAN THE TERRIBLE: Actually he had sex once. That's how he got his nickname.

GUNTHUR TOODY: If you have any idea whatsoever who Gunthur Toody was, you'll understand why he never had sex.

SANDRA DEE: Became pregnant in *A Summer Place* not from actually having sex, but from French kissing while lying down with Troy Donahue, which was known to cause pregnancies before 1964.

COLONEL SANDERS: Too busy chasing chickens around with an ax in his hand.

HELEN OF TROY: Helen Ripplemeyer, old maid country store owner in Troy, Alabama, that is.

One day, a traveling salesman came into her store. He had been stung on the end of his business by a yellow jacket and it had swollen to three times its original size.

He unveiled his painful privates to Helen Ripplemeyer and said, "What can you give me for this?"

Without a moment's hesitation, Miss Ripplemeyer replied, "How about a '48 Packard, the store and three acres of land?"

The traveling salesman left in a panic and Helen was never the same afterwards, spending her time with her cats and lusting privately for television wrestlers.

I guess that about covers it, but you may be wondering, if none of these people ever had sex, how did they work off their sexual energy?

In other words, if there ever was a time Richard Nixon felt a burning sensation in his loins, what did he do to put out the fire?

I'm just guessing here, but Nixon seems like the kind of guy who probably took a lot of cold showers in his time. His suits shrank after getting wet, of course, but it probably worked a lot better than going downstairs to the White House bowling alley and rolling a few frames with Haldeman and Ehrlichman.

As for Jerry Falwell, he went around screaming, "Kill the fornicators!" and sitting in the tenor chairs in the choir box.

34

If somebody wants to abstain from sex, either by choice or because they're weird like Nixon, that, of course, is fine with me. With the AIDS threat, we may see more abstinence in the future and there must be ways for all of us to transfer the powerful desire for sex toward something that offers at least some degree of relief.

There is masturbation, but studies by several million mothers over the years have found that a possible detriment to eyesight. Pearl Optical might disagree vehemently with this statement, but if a person who takes part in self-stimulation does begin to notice blurred vision (or the appearance of warts), it probably would be wise to seek some other form of sexual release.

Often during my sexually active years, I have had to abstain. Not by my own choice, but because there have been periods where it seemed the entire female population had banded together to force me into abstinence.

I've tried my share of cold showers, too, but I also found several other techniques that have allowed me to work off the, for lack of a better term, hots. For example:

GETTING SOMEBODY ELSE TO SHAMPOO YOUR HAIR: Nothing like it. It's sensuous, it's relaxing, and, if you keep your eyes tightly closed, completely pain-free. If you can convince the person doing the shampooing to get naked in the shower with you and all you still desire is a shampoo, it might be wise to seek professional help, however.

DOVE BARS: Dove Bars, a huge chunk of rich ice cream with sinfully delicious chocolate poured over it, will take your mind off sex every time.

If you are aroused more than normal, then eat six or seven Dove Bars. Do it in the closet to make the act seem even more forbidden.

GET SOMEBODY TO RUB YOUR BACK: Clean, relaxing, and you don't have to talk when you're through.

KILL A SLOTH: It seemed to work for Conan the Barbarian.

FOLD, SPINDLE AND MUTILATE A COMPUTER CARD: You kinky devil.

GET NAKED AND CLIMB UP A TREE: Make certain there aren't a lot of squirrels around, however. The little boogers bite.

DRIVE THROUGH A MCDONALD'S AND WHEN THEY ASK FOR YOUR ORDER SAY SOMETHING OBSCENE: After which, of course, the person on the other end will ask, "Would you like french fries with that?"

MAKE AN EARLY WITHDRAWAL FROM YOUR CERTIFICATE OF DEPOSIT ACCOUNT: This is if you're into pain. The substantial penalty for doing the above is Wilma from the bank comes over to your house and flogs you with a large roll of quarters.

TAKE A BATH IN ALKA-SELTZER: You'd be surprised what pleasure that much fizz can render.

FIND SOME MUD AND WIGGLE YOUR TOES IN IT: It is a little-known fact that between the toes are some of the most sensitive places on the human body. If this doesn't work for you at first, take off your shoes, stupid.

STOMP SOME ANTS: Even if it doesn't ease your sexual tension it could lead to a profitable career as an insect exterminator.

GET A HOBBY: This is probably the best known means to release sexual tension. There are many hobbies one can begin with very little money involved, including running rabbits, biting the heads off chickens at county fairs, rolling winos, toenail sculpture, competitive apple-bobbing, making up nasty rumors about people you hate, making funny sounds with your armpit, and building scale replicas of famous buildings using only a box of Mueller's Spaghetti.

If cost is no object, then maybe you can take up golf. Golf is a lot like sex, as a matter of fact. A wise person once said, "You don't have to be very good at either one to have fun."

Even with all that, however, a man is still going to think about sex occasionally—say when the *Sports Illustrated* swimsuit edition arrives.

The problem many men have is they get sexual urges, and the primary physical manifestation of the urges, at the worst possible time, such as while traveling on a public transport, while sitting around the pool, or while hanging sheetrock, for that matter.

This, of course, can be terribly embarrassing.

The key, when a man finds himself in such a situation, is to turn his mind toward matters that are totally asexual.

I've used Harry Truman a great deal. There is absolutely no way to continue to be sexually aroused when one is thinking of Harry Truman.

Think about that big hat he wore, about the Truman Doctrine, or about his rather plain, piano-playing daughter, Margaret.

If you find yourself still somewhat aroused after thinking about Harry Truman, try Herbert Hoover or even Millard Fillmore. That ought to do it.

This also can be helpful while in the midst of sex. One of the most difficult tasks a man has during sex is, no matter how much he tries, he often cannot avoid finishing before his partner, thus embarrassing himself and disappointing his partner.

When a man feels his passion getting out of control,

he can use Give 'Em Hell Harry or any of these asexual subjects:

Indiana. I can't think of anything that is sexy about the state of Indiana.

English peas. I detest English peas. Anybody who can obtain a sexual climax while thinking of English peas is a sick person.

The Atlanta Braves. This team is to baseball what Marjorie Main was to sex.

Your next visit to your mother-in-law's. Unless your mother-in-law still does a stage act involving poodles.

The Mormon Tabernacle Choir. If it weren't for having their own choir, Mormons would have even more babies.

The Sopwith Camel. But not the Fokker.

Betty Ann Cobblehammer. A girl in my school who had a flat nose, thick glasses, stringy hair, wore Dee Cee overalls and started dipping snuff when she was eleven.

Just think of snuff, for that matter.

Hemorrhoid medicine commercials. "Be sure to use only as directed." What do they think I'm going to do with that stuff, put it on a Saltine cracker and eat it?

Not me. I don't want to shrink up and be a little guy with little arms and legs.

Your next visit to your dentist. On second thought, don't think of that. The first dirty movie I ever saw was in a friend's trailer in college. For a buck, he showed *Tillie Goes to the Dentist for a Filling and a Drilling*.

The more you get into an exercise like this, the more you realize just how many asexual things there are. I tried to think of the most asexual element in our society.

I came up with bowling, despite the fact that "alley" and "gutter" are a part of bowling lingo and perhaps there is something about the way you hold a bowling ball that would conjure sexual thoughts. But you'd have to be pretty desperate for that to happen.

In the first place, Betty Ann Cobblehammer was a bowler. She rolled the ball with such speed she made a strike one day and one of the pins knocked a pin-boy unconscious three lanes over.

In the second place, when you bowl you have to wear one of those bowling shirts that are silk and have "Al's Bait and Tackle Shop" stitched on the back and the bowler's name (bowlers have names like Roger, Frank, Buck, Mildred, Bettye, Dedra, and Beatrice) written on the front pocket.

A bowling shirt is probably the least sexy of any

article of clothing, with the possible exception of a go-
rilla outfit or a pale blue polyester leisure suit worn
with a shirt that has pictures of pelicans on it.

Plus, as far as I know, there haven't been any bowling sex scandals.

And that's too bad, when you think about it. Can't
you imagine some great headlines that the *New York
Post* might run if, say, an investigation unearthed the
fact that **Jerry F**alwell had been having an illicit relationship with a lady bowler?

"FALWELL AND BOWLER—SEX IN THE GUTTER." Or,
"FALWELL STRIKES IN ALLEY"

And think about bowling shoes. They're uglier than
a pair of Thom McAn fruit boots or those shoes that
you can order in the mail from VFW magazines. I think
you could put Kim Basinger in a pair of bowling shoes
and have her be otherwise undraped and she couldn't
get Mickey Rourke to look at her twice.

Of course, Mickey Rourke, or any other man, would
have the good sense to say, "Kim, sweetheart, outta the
bowling shoes, pronto, and I'm not responsible for anything that happens after that."

I once was on a train with a group of lady bowlers.
The train was traveling between Chicago and Washington. Somewhere along the way, we picked up a
group of women on their way to Cincinnati for a bowling tournament.

I was sitting in the club car when they arrived. There

were maybe twenty of them. None looked like Kim Basinger, but there was one that reminded me of Hulk Hogan and another who had only two teeth, one on each side of her mouth.

"My god," I said to myself. "The woman is a walking seven–ten split."

The women bowlers sat themselves down, ordered beers, and then one opened up a cheese ball and they passed it around. Seven-ten had to sort of gum hers.

There are some women you can drink pretty. What I mean is that the more a man drinks, the larger his cull factor becomes and a woman he wouldn't have after two beers might become the object of his attention after ten.

I don't think it's possible to drink women bowlers pretty, but I did find out during the train ride that women bowlers do have at least some interest in sex.

I began to talk to some of the ladies as the beers settled in and loosened my inhibitions and fears (we're talking about rather large women here, several of whom had mustaches).

As I arose to excuse myself to the restroom, Seven-ten asked, "Where you goin', pretty thang?"

"To the rest room," I said.

"Didn't your doctor tell you not to do no heavy liftin'?" she asked, as the others laughed.

I went immediately to my roomette and locked the door. Seven-ten had that look in her eye.

When I finally emerged from my hiding place, we had passed Cincinnati and the lady bowlers had gotten off the train.

And what is strange is, to this day, every time I see sportscaster Chris Schenkel on television, I get an irresistible craving for cheese.

Perhaps the reason people bowl in the first place is because they have dull sex lives or aren't interested in sex anymore. Otherwise, why would anybody bowl?

First of all, a bowling ball is too heavy. One of the major causes of foot injury in this country is from people dropping bowling balls on one of their feet. A man from Cheyenne, Wyoming, tortured his wife by dropping his bowling ball on her feet every night after watching *Wheel of Fortune* on television.

I read about the incident in one of those newspapers they sell in the checkout line at grocery stores. The wife finally tired of this abuse, incidentally, and ground up her husband's bowling ball in the Cuisinart and fed it to him in a large bowl of chili, which prompted another story in one of those papers headlined, "I GROUND UP MY HUSBAND'S BOWLING BALL IN THE CUISINART AND FED IT TO HIM IN A BOWL OF CHILI," which was displayed next to another story headlined "ELVIS' GHOST APPEARS AT WAFFLE HOUSE."

It is also difficult to learn to keep score in bowling and there is virtually no way to cheat in bowling, short of dropping your ball on your opponent's foot, or if you are bowling for beer, on his head.

Fortunately for myself and others of my age group and rearing, we are used to doing without sex for long periods of time, and if we had to, we certainly could do it again.

As I grew into adulthood in the '50s and early '60s, I was surrounded by virginity. I knew this to be true because all the girls wore "virgin pins"—circular bits of jewelry attached to the front of a sweater or blouse —and were all saving themselves for their husbands, the poor, tortured devils who had to watch Jane Russell and Diana Dors on the movie screens of the day and then date the Flying Nun.

The closest you could get to sex with the girls of my youth was taking them to the drive-in movie and seeing how much you could get away with in the area of French kissing (speaking in tongues, as a manner of speaking), and touching south of her neck.

Unless you had dated a girl for at least a year, had promised to marry her and showered her with gifts like Evening in Paris perfume sets and seashells you picked up when you were in Daytona Beach with your parents, you probably weren't going to get any further down than the breast area, and you had to work at that with much dedication and stubbornness.

The favorite approach one could take in an effort to fondle his date's breast was THE SHOULDER ROUTE.

Normally, after a couple of dates, you could put your arm around a girl's shoulder with little or no reluctance on her part.

Getting to the breast was the logical step from there. Long arms were a tremendous benefit in this approach. You draped the arm over the girl's shoulder, and slowly moved your hand closer to the target.

It is approximately eight inches from the average-sized female's shoulder to the top of her breast. Even so, each bit of gained ground had to be taken in a casual, nondeliberate manner.

Were you to use the blitzkrieg method and simply all of a sudden grab a handful of breast, your date would be caught off guard and could react in any number of ways, including slapping, scratching or biting you, calling her brother Bruno to put your nose over by one of your ears, or pouring her Cherry Coke over the top of your head. Any of those occurrences could kill a romantic atmosphere in a heartbeat.

But by your taking it slowly and sneaking up on your target, rather than charging at it willy-nilly, the girl had time to adjust to the fact that she might be about to have her breasts touched, and decide whether or not you were worthy of such an honor and how long she would allow you this pleasure before she said, "Stop it! What kind of a girl do you think I am?"

At some point a young woman always asked this if any level of petting was taking place. How long after such petting began and she uttered that statement could run anywhere from three minutes to three hours.

The next step after fondling a breast from the outside was to get your hands on one of those things. This, however, was a goal very few of us ever reached in the years between 1956, when I was watching a ladies wrestling match on television and Kitty Bollita, the ladies' champion at the time, lost the top of her tights during a vicious dropkick, thus introducing me to the wonders of the female bosom, and 1966, when I got married for the first time and could have all the sex I wanted once a month, as long as I didn't tell anybody, we kept the lights off, her parents were not asleep in the next room, and the dog wasn't looking.

But even those who were fortunate enough to be granted such a favor as actually touching a girl's breasts returned from that to inform the rest of us that it required a great deal of pleading and the mechanical skills of a cat burglar.

"I'd been working on Marsha for six months," a friend was telling me. "Finally, last Friday night at the drive-in, she told me I could touch one of her knockers during intermission."

"Only one?" I asked, trembling with anticipation for the rest of the story.

"I get the other one if we get engaged," my friend said. (Before the sexual revolution, breasts were a favorite bargaining tool. God only knows how many promises were made in return for a handful of heaven.)

My friend then went on to explain the horrifying problem he encountered when he attempted to unfasten Marsha's bra.

"Houdini couldn't have gotten in there any faster than I did," my friend explained.

"Marsha kept saying, 'Hurry up. Intermission's almost over and I'm not going to miss one minute of *Gidget.* My whole life was flashing in front of my face. Here was the chance of a lifetime and she's wearing a bra you couldn't loose with an acetylene torch."

"What did you do?" I asked my friend.

"I took out my pocket knife and cut my way through."

"Which one did you get to touch?" I went on, not at all embarrassed at my intrigue.

"The left one," said my friend. "I named it Jake, and the other one Jesse after my uncle's bird dogs."

If we were nothing else in those days, at least we were romantic. Jake and Jesse were the two finest bird dogs in the county.

Besides married men, the only other males to have sex in my hometown before say, 1970, when girls cut all the pretenses and quit wearing bras at all, were those who were old enough to drive and to take out Rhonda Gentry. (Not her real name. Rhonda went on to a successful career with Mary Kay Cosmetics and I would not want knowledge of her background to hurt her in the business world.)

All I ever knew about Rhonda came to me second-hand, as I lay mired in that awkward age when it's not cool to still be riding a bicycle, but how are you going to get around otherwise when you're still two birthdays away from your driver's license?

Legend had it Rhonda could be convinced to do most anything within the limits of the imaginations of those much simpler times when kinky meant lighting both partner's cigarettes with one match after the party was over.

All Rhonda ever really expected in return for her favors was for someone to buy her a chocolate shake and a cheeseburger at the Dairy Queen before taking her home, and occasionally providing her with good seats for the Friday night wrestling matches at the VFW.

Rhonda was only slightly overweight and if the moon wasn't bright, she looked half pretty in the backseat of a '57 Chevy or a Nash, one of those that had the seats that folded back into a bed.

Her daddy worked the third shift at the mill, and her mama drank heavily, which made it easy for Rhonda to get out of the house.

I'm not certain why Rhonda decided to be sexually promiscuous in times when that was quite rare, but I think it had to do with the fact she loved and wanted to marry The Lone Strangler, a wrestler who wore a mask and was famous for his stranglehold, which sent many an opponent to the mat for the three count on Friday nights.

Rhonda always took Fridays off from the boys in town, dolled and powdered and perfumed herself and sat in the front row to watch The Lone Strangler. She urged him on with such suggestions as "Gouge his eyes out, Lone!," "Kick him in his business!" and "Pull out his tonsils for me, sugar!"

It is not known whether Rhonda and the Lone Strangler ever did it, but one of the Hadly boys got surly with her once for reasons unknown and punched her a couple of times. Witnesses said Rhonda promptly put a stranglehold on him that would have made Lone proud, and talk was anybody who could get the Lone Strangler to show somebody his famous hold must have been getting *something* in return.

To understand the importance of young ladies like Rhonda back in simpler times, I offer the following incident.

A Shakespearean troupe on its way to do King Lear *in Dothan, Alabama, was going through town one day when the bus in which it was traveling slung a rod.*

Hamp Turnipseed, the local mechanic, said it would take a day to repair the bus. Townspeople opened their arms to these travelers and invited them into their homes for dinner and breakfast and a place to spend the night.

So grateful was the troupe, out of Ooltewah, Tennessee—just outside Chattanooga—it decided to perform Macbeth for the community in the local school cafetorium. The only problem was that the actress who was to play Lady Macbeth had been overcome by the intense heat of the afternoon and was not able to perform.

Little did we know that Rhonda had secret aspirations to be an actress on the stage. She volunteered for the part and the troupe's director gave it to her.

In the climactic scene, Macbeth took out his sword and ran Rhonda through. She fell to the stage floor in what we all thought was quite a professional manner. Even the back row shook from the collision.

The actor playing Macbeth gave his ensuing line: "Forsooth! What have I done?" We could all see he was indeed repentant over his action.

Just then, Hamp Turnipseed walked in to tell the director how he was coming with the bus. When he saw what had happened and heard Macbeth's line, he bellowed, "I'll tell you what you did, you son of a bitch. You've killed the only whore this side of the Alabama line."

I won't bore you with any intimate details of my early sex life, such as it was. Those first-time stories are generally overdone, and who wants to hear them in the first place?

What I will say, however, is that sex was on my mind a great deal when I was a child, and don't think if you have children they aren't the same. In fact, they probably think about sex even more than I did because I didn't have cable television, commercials discussing "maxi-pads," and music videos that could stir up youthful hormones in five states.

About all I had was the Sears, Roebuck catalog, the dictionary and the aforementioned occasional sex novel someone had pilfered from his father's socks drawer, and the *National Geographic*.

As soon as the new Sears, Roebuck catalog came, my grandfather and I would sit down and look at the pictures of shotguns and garden tractors.

As soon as he tired of looking at shotguns and garden tractors, I would promptly return to the scuppernong vines—my personal den of iniquity—and turn to the ladies' underwear section.

Most of the women who posed for the catalog, by modern standards, were ugly and a bit overweight. But I had my imagination. Later, I would have the opportunity to go into bars where young ladies danced in the absolute and glorious nude, but there is truth to the idea that sexiness is best accomplished with a tease.

I also used the dictionary in order to pique my sexual interest by looking up dirty words, or words I thought at the time were dirty. You didn't see these words in print in newspapers or textbooks back then. These were mostly anatomical terms I would spring on my friends who either didn't have a dictionary at their homes or were not as sexually aware as myself and hadn't thought to look these words up.

After all those efforts to look up dirty words in practically every dictionary I came across, I never did strike gold. I never found the "F" word, *the* dirty word of all dirty words. Unabridged, my fanny.

But my efforts did lead me to the knowledge of a great many words I never would have been able to add to my vocabulary. Here are some examples:

1. "Fucoid"—of or like seaweed

2. "Fugger"—German family of merchants and bankers of the fifteenth to nineteenth centuries

3. "Fug"—the heavy air in a closed room, regarded as either oppressive and murky or warm and cozy

4. "Fukien"—province of southeast China on Taiwan Strait.

One night over dinner, when I was about twelve, and had spent a good portion of the afternoon looking for dirty words in my dictionary, I said:

"Well, I guess everybody heard about the Fuggers

eating all that fucoid, and how they had to endure all the fug on their way to Fukien."

My grandmother fainted, and my mother took away my dictionary rights for a year.

The *National Geographic*, of course, has been used for years as a means for young people to get a clean shot at the human anatomy, thanks to the hundreds of pictorials *NG* has done regarding the lifestyle of still-primitive cultures in general, those where the women go around with no tops on in particular.

In my school, however, the librarian noticed how quickly the sections of the *Geographic* that featured the topless native women became frayed and dog-eared.

After that, when the new magazines arrived at school each month, she would go through *NG* with a pair of scissors and cut out all the good stuff and leave in the sections with close-up photographs of humming-birds and one-cellular sea life. I lost all interest in geography after that. It seemed pointless.

Anyway, I'm really not certain how we started with Richard Nixon and got all way to the *National Geographic* in one chapter, but it was necessary for the following reasons:

—Since this is a book about sex and Richard Nixon never had sex, we won't have to mention him another single time, which should encourage the reader to go forward.

—I had a chance to make fun of Jerry Falwell, which I always attempt to do every chance I get. The man is boring and pompous and must have something on Ted Koppel, when one considers how many times he has been on *Nightline* making imbecilic comments. I reserve the right to say other bad things about Falwell as we go along and I think of more.

—I needed to point out that we are living in a unique sexual period: Society certainly has loosened its sexual regulations over the past several years, but the threat of disease may force us back into the sexual situation I knew growing up. Rhonda Gentry, come back, wherever you are.

—I wanted to make certain everybody knew you could have lots of sexual fun with a dictionary but you must give the fugger a chance.

CHAPTER THREE

I had the urge to entitle this chapter "Sex on the Road," but it sounded too much like a cheap novel that would be on sale at truck stops, the sort that sell those little wooden plaques with the picture of a barefoot girl who is saying, "I Should Have *Danced* All Night."

I feel I also should point out I have never had sex at either a bus station or a truck stop, but I did have a friend once who claimed to have had sex with a girl while riding the Tilt-a-Whirl at a carnival in Panama City, Florida.

"Is it difficult to have sex in the "Tilt-A-Whirl?" I asked my friend.

"Ever try buttering a hot biscuit in a clothes dryer at the laundromat?" he asked.

I supposed when he told me that, he had made a perfectly sensible analogy. We were drinking heavily at the time, however—vodka tonics (it was summer)—and some years later, perfectly sober, I tried to butter a hot biscuit in a clothes dryer down at the laundromat, and once I got the biscuit open, it wasn't all that hard to butter it as long as I kept my head still.

Once I got out of the dryer and my head quit spinning, I decided a much better analogy to making love in the Tilt-a-Whirl in Panama City would be trying to hold on to a greased pig during an earthquake.

At any rate, this chapter is about some of my sexual experiences while traveling, but instead of "Sex on the Road," I have decided to entitle this chapter "By the Time I Get to Myrtle Beach She'll Be Completely Out of the Mood."

Allow me to begin by saying I am an expert on road sex. That is because I have been on a large number of regular honeymoons, several second honeymoons and even a few of what I call "practice honeymoons," where you, well, practice so in case you ever have a regular honeymoon there won't be any surprises, which brings up a honeymoon joke:

There was a black guy and a white guy who were best of friends all the way back to childhood. Both were great athletes, but the white guy always came out ahead of his black friend by the slightest of margins.

When they were in Little League, the black kid hit .450. The white kid hit .456. In high school, the black kid was all-region tailback. His white friend was all-state quarterback.

They went to the same college. The black guy was all-conference tailback and most valuable player in the Orange Bowl. His white friend was all-America at quarterback and won the Heisman Trophy.

It was the same with marriage. The black guy married Miss New York. The white guy married Miss America, whose father owned a liquor store.

The two friends decided to honeymoon in Hawaii together. The two couples arrived, checked into their hotel and the two men decided to meet in the lounge for a drink. There, the black friend challenged his pal:

"Listen," he began, "you've always beaten me out by just a little in everything we've ever done.

"But I know there's one thing whites can't do as well as blacks and that's make love. I'll bet you a hundred bucks I make love more times on my honeymoon night than you will."

The white friend took the challenge and asked, "But how are we going to know who's made love the most?"

"Simple," the other friend said. "Just write the number of times on your bathroom mirror with a piece of soap and we'll compare them in the morning."

The two friends finished their cocktails and then joined their brides in their respective rooms. The white guy ordered champagne and after he and his wife had finished a few glasses, they made wild and passionate love.

The husband then went into the bathroom and made a mark on the bathroom window with a bar of soap. He returned to the bedroom and made passionate love to his wife again.

Afterward, he slipped back into the bathroom and made another mark next to the previous one. After a third lovemaking session, he put a third mark next to the other two and then drifted off to sleep.

The next morning, the two pals had breakfast together.

"I know I got you this time!" said the black guy. "No way you could keep up with the performance I put on last night."

His friend grinned. "Don't be too certain."

"Did you keep score?" he was asked.

"Right on the bathroom mirror, just like you said."

The two friends immediately went up to the white guy's room and walked into the bathroom.

The black guy saw the three soap marks on the mirror and said, "I don't believe it. You've beaten me again."

The white guy said, "By how much?"

The black guy looked at the mirror again and answered, "A hundred and eleven to thirty-eight."

My first honeymoon occurred in 1966, with my first wife, which is how normal things worked out back then before men starting wearing earrings.

We married in my hometown church in Moreland, Georgia, and left afterwards for Myrtle Beach, South Carolina, a trip of some eight hours. It was July.

I drove us in our 1965 Volkswagen Beetle, the one the gasoline pedal had fallen off of, the one with no air conditioning, and the one with all the empty beer cans inside.

I remain convinced that if you throw two empty beer cans into the back of a car, they immediately will mate, and all of a sudden, there are seventy-five empty beer cans in the back of your car. The same theory applies to tennis balls, old newspapers, and candy wrappers. Put two of any of them in the backseat floorboard of a car and they will multiply with frightening speed.

We arrived in Myrtle Beach for our honeymoon night, tired and hot.

"Where are we staying?" my new bride asked me.

"I'll find a place," I said.

"We don't have reservations?"

"I forgot to make any."

"Let me see if I have this straight," she said. "We've been on the road for eight hours in this trash heap, and we don't have anywhere to sleep on our honeymoon night? This can't be happening to me."

"Relax," I assured her, "I'll find a place."

And find a place I did. Three hours later at two o'clock in the morning at the Sea Horse Inn, fifteen blocks from the beach, but quite convenient to a discount tire store across the street.

"Do you notice something strange about this room?" my wife asked after I had brought in the last bag.

"As a matter of fact I do," I said. "The towels in the bathroom say 'Holiday Inn.' "

"Guess again, Conrad Hilton," she went on. "There isn't a bed in this room."

"That can't be," I said. "I paid six dollars."

I went back and woke up the desk clerk, a tiny little man with hair growing out of his ears, and told him of the missing bed in our room. He seemed quite upset to be roused from his chair where he was sleeping with a folded copy of *The Police Gazette* on his lap.

"A bed's sort of crucial," I said. "It's our wedding night."

The man grunted. I hate a man who grunts. When one grunts, it indicates one obviously is displeased and isn't the least bit concerned with your plight, even if you are faced with spending your wedding night on the floor of a seedy motel where they'd probably steal *your* towels if you had any.

"The bed's in the wall," the man said after he stopped grunting.

I went back to the room.

"The bed's in the wall," I said to my wife.

She grunted.

I pulled the bed out of the wall, and turned the covers back. My wife went into the bathroom to do whatever it is women do in a bathroom just before they are to have sex.

(I have often suspected that in my case, they go in there to give themselves a pep talk: "You've got to do this," they say to the mirror. "There absolutely is no way out of this. Go back in there and pretend you're having a good time. It won't last over three minutes at the outside.")

My wife returned to our wedding night bed, wearing a black, lacy thing, most of which was missing. I took her into my arms and kissed her passionately, at which the time the air conditioning unit in the window made a sound much like a pulpwood truck does when it is being cranked on a cold morning.

"What was that!" shrieked my wife.

I wasn't sure. I turned the lights back on and looked outside for a pulpwood truck. There wasn't one, so I decided it had been the air conditioning unit.

I turned off the lights again, and again I embraced my bride. That's when the cricket started making the sound a cricket makes.

"There's a cricket in this bed," insisted my wife.

I turned the lights back on and we both got out of bed. I pulled the covers off, but I couldn't find the cricket. I looked under the bed and still no cricket.

By now, it's after three in the morning on my wedding night and I'm searching for a cricket that may, or may not, exist. I can feel my own passion draining away. Meanwhile, my wife has gone back into the bathroom for what I figure is a Lord-give-me-strength session with the mirror.

I never did find the cricket. Mercifully, it finally stopped cricketing shortly after four. My wife had returned from the bathroom with metal things in her hair and a greasy ingredient all over her face. We talked for a while, about how nice the wedding had been and how her aunt Mavis looked since she'd lost all that weight and our exhaustion finally took us and we slept, her on her side, me nestled against her back, my nose caught in one of those metal things in her hair.

It did get better. We found a nicer place to stay the next day, and I won a watch playing bingo and we went out to a nice restaurant with a band in the bar. We asked the band to play Frank and Nancy Sinatra's "Something Special," our song, and when we got back to our motel room that night, we had our first three minutes of marital bliss.

Ten months later, we stepped into our quarters on what seemed to be the boiler level of the *S.S. Paradise* for our second honeymoon.

"When you booked this compartment," my wife asked, "did you know we were going to have bunk beds?"

I swore that I hadn't.

We went on our second honeymoon because our first one had, in effect, been a complete failure. The watch I won in bingo quit running a few days after I got back home, and my wife ate something that gave her diarrhea and she spent the last three days of our original honeymoon in the bathroom. There are an awful lot of things that will knock sexuality for a complete loop, and diarrhea ranks right up there.

Neither my wife nor I had ever been out of the country, so we picked Nassau in which to second honeymoon. We rode the train from Atlanta to Miami to catch the *S.S. Paradise.*

"You'll love riding the train," I said to my wife.

"If it's anything like riding in your rolling Dempsy Dumpster to Myrtle Beach, I can't wait," she replied.

The primary reason my first marriage didn't work was because my wife was not a forgiving person.

I didn't know the train was going to be four hours late. I couldn't afford a sleeper and we had to spend the night in the coach next to a man who coughed a lot. I didn't know the ladies' restroom would smell as bad as my wife insisted it did.

"My god," she said, "I'm on the 'Train to Hell.' "

We arrived in Miami eight hours late, and took a taxi to the debarkation point of our cruise. The cab driver was surly. What I remember more than that was he had a little dab of saliva stuck on the corner of his mouth. No matter how much he scowled, it just sat there.

I handed the driver a five at the end of the trip and stood waiting patiently for my change. When the driver handed it to me, I put it in my pocket.

"No tip?" he asked, disdainfully.

"Here's a tip," I said. "Never go out in the rain without your galoshes."

The cab driver started to get out of the car, at which time I grabbed my stomach as if I were about to throw up.

Pretending to be about ready to throw up will get you out of a lot of tight spots while traveling. I am certain James Bond used that tactic more than once.

I enjoyed our little trip to Nassau. My wife bought a wood carving and a basket. I bought some rum. We learned to fit ourselves in the bottom bunk with only a slight amount of discomfort, tried to make love several times and succeeded once, and I learned all the words to "Yellow Bird."

But as the trip grew longer, I began to feel an occasional pang of homesickness. Having never been out of the United States before, I also began to feel an inkling of uneasiness.

What if I got sick, I asked myself. I wasn't certain if they had doctors in the Bahamas or not, but if they did, what sort of treatment could I expect? Do they practice voodoo here?

I could see myself, doubled over with pain from an attack of appendicitis or something like that, being led into a thatch hut with a lot of native women around with their breasts exposed. (I had been an avid reader of *National Geographic* for years, which you'd know if you read Chapter 2.)

And once inside the hut, they would make me drink some potion made out of lizard blood and then the native women would dance around the hut, chanting while their breasts flopped up and down. Then, a witch doctor would come into the hut and shake something that rattled at me and, meanwhile, my side is killing me and there is no phone, so I have to stay there and despite all the rattling and breast-flopping, I die from a ruptured appendix and never get back home to watch *The Dating Game* and *Arrest and Trial,* my two favorite TV shows at the time.

And what if I got arrested in a foreign country? I'd seen those black and white movies before.

They haul you into a tiny police station with a ceiling fan where a little man with hair growing out of his ears says, "Your papers, please," and you say, "Gosh, I didn't know I was supposed to have any papers, I'm here with my wife and she's gone shopping for wood carvings and baskets."

And the little man grunts and they put you in a cell with a witch doctor they just arrested for malpractice, one murderer, two rapists, three people who didn't fill their customs forms out correctly, and Frankie Garfield, the school bully who used to beat me up in the fourth grade. What he would be doing there I have no idea, but nightmares rarely make a lot of sense.

And what if a war broke out between the U.S. and the Bahamas? Lyndon Johnson was in the White House. Anything could happen. They would arrest all United States citizens and put us in some sort of camp with barbed wire around it and we would have to stay there until the war was over and miss the World Series.

I became so frightened of these possibilities, I refused to leave the ship for the last two days of the trip and stayed at the ship's bar and drank beer. I met a guy who was vacationing ("on holiday") from England who said he was a socialist and America had no business in Vietnam, which made me even more homesick.

My wife, of course, thought I was crazy to have such fears.

"You're not going to get sick, you're not going to be arrested, and we certainly aren't going to get in a war with the Bahamas, you idiot," she assured me.

Still, when I first spotted land on our return trip to Miami, I burst into "God Bless America," at which time my wife became quite embarrassed and crawled under a blanket on one of the deck chairs and refused to acknowledge any sort of connection with me until we got back on the train in Miami, when she pointed out my various shortcomings until she finally went to sleep somewhere on the outskirts of Palatka.

That was the end of honeymoons for my first wife and me. We got a divorce a few months later. But we had our times. Perhaps we hadn't had sex in a Tilt-a-Whirl, but we did it once in the back of that VW Beetle with all the beer cans rolling around. Two cats fighting in a trash can in the alley didn't make half the noise we did.

When I divorced the first Mrs. Grizzard I was twenty-three, and had been appointed assistant sports editor of the *Atlanta Journal,* a thankless task that involved getting to the paper at five each morning and seeing to it that the *Journal* had a good sports section that afternoon, despite the fact that the assistant sports editor, not to mention most of the rest of the staff, were suffering from hangovers.

The assistant sports editor never got to do anything exciting, such as going out of town to cover a sporting event. That is, except one time a year when the baseball writer took his vacation. The assistant sports editor got to take the baseball writer's place on a road trip.

In 1970, the Atlanta Braves were, as they have been most years, horrendous. Their manager was a man named Luman Harris, who hated sportswriters. His pitching coach was a man named Harry Dorish.

During one game, Harris phoned Dorish in the bullpen and said, "Harry, get a lefthander ready."

Dorish replied, "How about McQueen?"

"No, Harry," said Harris. "He's already in the game."

The traveling secretary of the team was a man named Donald Davidson, who was a midget and cursed a lot, especially when he had been drinking. One night, he and Joe Torre, then a Braves player, were drinking in a bar and they became loud and a bit too foul-mouthed for folks at a table near them.

"Please," said a man at the other table, "Can you stop using such language?"

Donald, who used the "w" sound for words beginning in "l," knew he had the burly Torre to defend him, so he hopped up on the man's table and began kicking drinks on the floor.

"Wangwage?" he screamed. "You want wangwage, I'll give you some wangwage!"

The people at the table got up immediately and left, and Donald sat back down with Torre and continued drinking.

I accompanied the Braves on a July road trip that included stops in Philadelphia, New York, and Montreal. The team was in last place, having exited the National League pennant race shortly after opening day.

The Braves played the Phillies in old Connie Mack

Stadium, which was located in a terrible part of Philadelphia where blacks had recently lynched a white man. The Braves lost three games to the Phillies, but nobody got lynched.

The other highlights of the trip were discovering that the bulge in Rico Carty's hip when he came to the plate was his wallet filled with $100 bills, getting to stay at the Bellevue Stratford Hotel, where Legionnaire's disease would first break out years later, and hearing Donald Davidson cuss out the bus driver who drove the team from the Philadelphia airport to the hotel because his girlfriend was on the bus.

"Get that bweeping bwoad off duh bweeping bus!" Donald screamed.

"She doesn't have another way home," the driver said.

"I don't give a bweep!" replied Donald.

The driver put his girlfriend off on the airport tarmac and left her there.

The Braves also lost three games to the Mets in New York. After the last game on Sunday, we boarded a flight to Montreal.

I didn't know much about Canada at the time, other than the fact that Canadians were big hockey fans, their football rules were screwed up, and fans had to sit through two national anthems—ours and theirs—before every baseball game at Park Jarry where Montreal's then-fledgling expansion team, the Expos, played.

(Later, there would be an expansion hockey team come to Atlanta, the Flames. I never could get a handle on hockey. I never could find the puck, for one thing. For another, I never could figure what "icing the puck" meant.

(My stepbrother, humorist Ludlow Porch, did, however, after watching a few hockey games, come up with a few ways to make it more interesting.

("First," he explained, "they should do away with the penalty box. If a player violates a rule, half his stick should be cut off. If he violates another, he has to relinquish one of his skates.)

About the only other thing I knew about Canada was that it is very cold there. In fact, I had even learned an old drinking toast about Canada. It went:

Here's to Canada,
Land of the snows,
But cold,
God knows.

What I didn't know was a lot of Canadians, the ones in Montreal especially, spoke French. We stayed at the Queen Elizabeth Hotel and each morning when I got my wake-up call, the operator would say both *"Bonjour"* and *"Good Morning."* I wrote to my mother about that.

What else I didn't know was that Canadians who spoke English said "ay" a lot, as in, "I'm about to freeze my butt off, ay," and "Let's grab a bottle of Labatt's, ay?" Labatt's being a beer.

We arrived in Montreal on Sunday night and the Braves had Monday off, which gave me two nights and two full days to see the city, and not to have to talk to baseball players.

Sunday night, I went to Joe's Steak House with a fellow writer and then we went to a bar where I struck up a conversation with a young lady who was vacationing (on holiday) from England and was a socialist who didn't think the U.S. should be in Vietnam.

"You have a brother who visits the Bahamas, ay?" I asked her. She eventually left with a guy wearing a beret.

The next morning, I decided to visit the shopping mall underneath the hotel. I needed some typing paper. I walked into a drugstore and asked a lovely young woman behind the counter, "I need some typing paper, ay?"

"Plain or onionskin?" she asked in a thick accent, indicating her French connection.

"Plain," I think I said. Because she was so attractive, I even forgot to put the "ay" on the end of it.

As she was putting my typing paper in a bag, I asked her name.

"Carole," she said.

Only she didn't say just "Carole" like a girl from Atlanta would say. She said, *"Karoool."*

She had black hair and dark skin. She had brown eyes and large breasts. She could dance topless around my thatch hut anytime, I said to myself.

Did I dare try to ask her out?

Here I was, alone in a foreign country. I had never dated anybody outside of Coweta County, Georgia, at the time, much less anybody from a country where their football fields were ten yards too long.

I decided to take a chance.

"Karool," I began, "this is my first time in Montreal. Could maybe you show me some of the city?"

There was a pause.

"Ay?" I added.

She giggled a petite giggle.

I had rounded first.

"And where are you from?" she asked me.

"Atlanta," I said. "That's in the U.S."

" 'Gone wiz ze Wind.' "

"Exactly."

"Are you, then, the Rhett Butler type, no?"

"Frankly, my dear," I answered, rolling now, "I would like to have dinner with you this very evening."

"That would be very nice," Karool said.

She gave me her address. I went and bought an ascot.

I'm not sure exactly why, but it probably had something to do with a David Niven movie I once saw.

Karool, the ascot and I had a wonderful romantic dinner together. She ordered something that came with lots of sauce on it. I ordered what I thought was chicken and turned out to be fish with a lot of tomatoes around it. I ate carefully so as not to get anything on my pants or ascot.

After wine—an arrogant but not offensive Bin No. 11 —we caught a horse-drawn carriage that took us to the top of Mont Tremblant. I was heady from the wine and the smell of Karool's perfume, dominant even over the smell of the horse, and quite intoxicating.

We had our first kiss. The earth trembled beneath the carriage. The horse had pulled us over a pothole in the road.

I saw Karool each night after the Braves' games, all of which they managed to lose.

(The team stayed loose, however, despite the losing streak. As we were waiting for the bus driver to take myself and the team to Park Jarry for a game, two of the players spotted a KLM flight attendant's bag sitting near a taxi stand. The flight attendant was not in sight.

(The players opened the bag and took out the flight attendant's dainty underthings. One tied her bra around his head, while the other held up a pair of red panties to the delight of the players still on the bus.

(Meanwhile, the bus driver didn't arrive for fifteen more minutes, and when he finally did arrive, Donald Davidson gave him one of his best tirades.

("You bweeping bweep!" said Donald. "You're fifteen minutes wate!"

(Unfortunately, the bus driver spoke only French, so the more Donald screamed at him, the more he smiled and nodded his head in agreement.

("I hate a bweeping country where every sonovabitch you see is a bweeping foreigner," was diplomat Davidson's eventual appraisal of the situation.)

I was maddened by love. Even when Luman Harris called me dirty names that outdid even Donald Davidson, it didn't matter. The name Karool danced unperturbed in my mind's eye, even when Larry Jaster told me to cram it up my hindparts when I asked him why he grooved a 3-0 pitch to Ron Fairly, which Fairly hit out of the park in the ninth inning for a grand slam home run, and a 7–4 Expos victory.

Karool met me at the airport before I boarded the charter home. We hugged and said we would write.

Before I walked into the tunnel leading to the gate, I turned and looked at her once more.

"Adieu, mon amie!" I said.

"Goodbye, Looeese," she answered.

"Get the bweep inside the plane," said Donald Davidson.

We did write. Long, adoring letters. I had two weeks

vacation in late August. I would return to my darling Karool and Montreal.

"Please come," she wrote when I advised her of my plans. "I am so lonely without you."

God.

I drove to Montreal in my 1968 Cutlass. I had sold the VW for eight cases of beer and a Jack Kramer tennis raquet.

The first day, I drove all the way from Atlanta to Wilkes-Barre, Pennsylvania. I left early the next morning and got closer and closer to Montreal and my beloved.

A man in the bar at the motel in Wilkes-Barre had told me about buying duty-free cigarettes at the Canadian border. I was on a limited budget. I made a mental note to buy myself a carton of Marlboros, which I smoked at the time.

I missed the trailer where they were selling the cigarettes, however, and drove up to Canadian customs. "Is this your first time in Canada?" the customs officer asked. "No," I said.

"How long will you be in Canada?" the customs officer asked me.

"Two weeks," I said.

"You are on business?"

"Pleasure. Her name is Karool."

The officer smiled.

"By the way," I said, "where do I buy the duty-free cigarettes."

"Oh, I am sorry," he said. "But you should have stopped at the trailer just behind you."

I started to back up.

"I am afraid," the officer said, "you cannot back up. You must drive around and back through United States Customs."

No problem. I did a quick U.

"Are you an American citizen?" the U.S. Customs officer asked me.

"Yes."

"And where were you born?"

"Fort Benning, Georgia."

"And where do you live?"

"Atlanta, Georgia."

"And how long have you been in Canada?"

I looked at my watch.

"About seventeen seconds," I said.

The officer did not seem amused, so I explained about the cigarettes.

He waved me through.

I bought the carton of Marlboros and pulled back into the Canadian customs line. The officer who greeted me was not the one with whom I had talked moments before.

"Have you ever been to Canada before?" he asked.

"Yes," I said.

"And when was that?"

I looked about my watch.

"About four minutes ago," I said.

He did not seem amused, either, so I told him about the cigarettes, too.

"May I see the cigarettes, please?" he asked.

I was stricken with terror. Suddenly, all my fears about being out of my country came back. What had I done wrong? Where would they take me? Would I be beaten? Would I ever see Karool again?

I handed the man the carton of cigarettes. He looked at them and handed them back to me.

"That is fine," he said. "Please continue."

"Well, King," I said, "does that mean this case is closed?"

Sgt. Preston of the Yukon had been one of the favorite television shows of my youth.

The customs officer glared at me. I drove away and made a mental note to myself never to be a smart aleck while trying to get into somebody else's country.

I arrived in Montreal in late afternoon and checked back into the Queen Elizabeth. It was Sunday, and Karool was not working in the drugstore. I called her at home.

"I am here!" I announced when she answered the phone.

There was a strange silence on the other end.

Then, Karool said, almost hesitantly, "That is good, Looeese."

"There's something wrong?" I asked, my heart pounding in anticipation of something horrid about to happen.

"I must talk to you," Karool said.

"I'll be right over."

She hugged me and she even kissed me. Then, she plunged a dagger deep into me.

"I wrote you last week, but you must have left before the letter arrived," she said.

"I never got a letter."

"Looeese," she went on. "What we have had together was very special, but it cannot continue."

"Go ahead and give it to me straight," I said. I heard David Niven say that to a woman once.

"I am engaged to be married." Karool gave it to me straight.

"Do what?" I asked.

"He is an old boyfriend," she explained. "We were together for a long time, and then he went away. Now he is back."

I slumped in my chair. I had just driven 1,200 miles to see my beloved Karool. I had been forced to spend a night in Wilkes-Barre, Pennsylvania, I had barely escaped through Canadian and U.S. Customs, and now she was telling me she was engaged?

I did the only manly thing I could do. I cried and I begged.

She wouldn't budge.

"Now," she said, "you had better go."

I drove back to my hotel. I was numb. I decided to do something else manly. Get drunk.

I went back to the same bar where I had met the lady from London on my trip to Montreal with the Braves. A black guy wearing a beret sat down next to me and said he was a socialist and America had no business in Vietnam.

I left Montreal at dawn. I suddenly hated the city. I hated Canada. I hated hockey. I hated fish with tomatoes on it and Ron Fairly and that dump of a Montreal ballpark, Park Jarry.

"Sgt. Preston was probably gay," I said to myself.

I pressed down on the gas pedal. Get me the hell back home! If I could just get back inside the U.S., I would feel a lot better.

Finally, the border.

I went through the usual with the U.S. Customs officer. Then, he spotted the carton of Marlboros in the backseat of my car. I hadn't been in Canada long enough to even open it.

"May I see the cigarettes, please?" he asked.

No. Please don't do this to me. The love of my life has just dumped me and all I want to do is get back to my precious country.

I handed the officer the carton of cigarettes. He looked at it and them said, "Please pull your car over and step inside."

Who was inside? Broderick Crawford with a billy stick?

Actually, it was just a minor thing. I had to pay the duty on the duty-free cigarettes I had purchased when I drove into Canada.

I made it as far as Carlisle, Pennsylvania, before stopping at the Carlisle Indian Inn. Jim Thorpe and all that.

The next day, I drove over to the Gettysburg National Battlefield and toured that. Pickett never had a chance.

I spent the next night in Hagerstown, Maryland. The next morning, I headed back toward Atlanta.

Ever since that experience, I have had a hard time liking anything that is Canadian. I pull against the Expos, even when they play the Mets. If I cared even the slightest for the American League, which I don't, I would hate the Toronto Blue Jays.

Canadians love hockey and they deserve to and I'm up to here with Canadians complaining about acid rain.

After all, Canadians are foreigners, and I think it was former Heisman Trophy winner George Rogers of the University of South Carolina who said it best when he was asked if he might play Canadian football after his college eligibility was up.

"No way," said George. "I'm not about to go overseas to play nothin'."

CHAPTER FOUR

When it comes to sex on a public conveyance, my interest lies primarily in the area of passenger trains.

You can have sex in a rickshaw, on a boat, in an automobile, of course, on a Greyhound bus, or even while piloting an airplane. (See Chapter 1.)

But trains. When it comes to sex on trains, I get my interest honestly.

I had an Uncle Junior who was a traveling salesman back in the '30s. He rode trains, and in his waning years he used to share train stories with me.

I remember my favorite:

"Son," Uncle Junior began, "Let me tell you about

the time I rode the old *Empire Builder* from Chicago to Seattle.

"I had settled into the lounge car somewhere west of Minneapolis when a lovely young woman, impeccably dressed and lightly perfumed, entered and sat next to me.

"I asked if I could buy her a drink and she said I could. After a round or two, I asked her, 'What's a lovely lady like you doing on the train all alone?'

"She replied, 'I'm a nymphomaniac and I've had sex in all the states except Montana, Idaho, and Washington.'

"I never blinked an eye," Uncle Junior continued.

"I said, 'I hope you won't find me too nosy, but a woman like you, who's obviously had a great deal of experience, might could answer this. What sort of men make the best lovers?'

" 'Cowboys,' she answered. 'Cowboys make wonderful lovers.'

" 'And who would be second? I went on.

" 'Jewish men,' she replied. 'Jewish men are quite good.'

"We rode on a few more miles and she said, 'You've asked me all these personal questions, and I don't know a thing about you. What's your name?'

" 'Proud to meet you, ma'am' I said. 'I'm Hopalong Ginsberg at your service.' "

If I was not actually conceived on a train, I think the

groundwork for my being was planted on a train. My mother once told me the story of meeting my father at Atlanta's Terminal Station when he returned home from World War II in 1945. They boarded another train, the *Man O' War,* for Columbus, Georgia, and Fort Benning, where my father had been ordered following the war.

Mother didn't give me every detail, but apparently she and my father did involve themselves in some sort of romantic efforts.

"Your daddy had been gone a long time," is how my mother explained it.

Anyway, when I am in or around a passenger train, I feel strangely close to my roots. Also, when people ask me what sign I was born under, I say it could have been the one that says, "Dining car in opposite direction."

I married a second time in 1973. It was sort of a rush job. One evening, she up and said, "Let's get married."

It sounded like the thing to do at the time. I phoned my stepbrother, Ludlow Porch, the radio star, and told him of my plans.

"Are you certain you know what you're doing?" he asked me.

"It's just that we have so much in common," I replied.

"Oh, she likes to hang out in bars all night, and play poker, too?"

"Cut the cute stuff," I said. "I need your help. We want to get married as soon as possible."

Ludlow worked miracles. He scheduled the wedding at his home, which was a good idea because I lived in an efficiency apartment at the time.

His wife and children decorated the house, hanging black crepe paper on the walls, as I recall. They also bought a cake from a local bakery, and since there was no time to purchase a ring, I used Ludlow's son's Boy Scout ring.

There was also the problem of a minister.

"It will be difficult to arrange for one on such short notice," Ludlow said.

"Handle it," I suggested, knowing that he most certainly would.

There was one other thing.

"While I arrange for the blood tests," I said to my stepbrother, "I want you to call Amtrak. I want to spend my honeymoon night on a train."

"Do what?" Ludlow inquired.

I didn't have time to go into all the reasons why, I just said, "I saw a movie once with Barbara Stanwyck and some guy and they spent their honeymoon night on a train. I simply think it would be quite romantic, a honeymoon to remember as we grow old together."

"Where do you want to go?" asked Ludlow.

I hadn't given that much thought.

"Florida," I said finally. "Get me on a train going someplace in Florida where it is nice and warm."

"Coach or sleeper?" he asked.

"Be serious," I said. "I'm not sitting out there with the coughers and throat-clearers in coach. Get me a deluxe bedroom."

There was trouble from the start. The minister Ludlow located to marry us wore a toupee, had a thin little moustache, and he rattled around in his suit, which would have fit him and three twelve-year-old boys.

"Where did you find the minister?" I asked Ludlow.

"Who did you want on such short notice?" he asked back. "Billy Graham?"

I continued to eye the minister as I attempted to figure out what he looked like. He certainly didn't look like any minister I had ever seen, but remember this was 1973, and I'd never seen Ernest Angsley back then.

Finally, I figured it out.

"The crooked Indian agent," I said to Ludlow.

"What are you talking about?"

"Brother whatever over there looks like a crooked Indian agent. Remember in the old western movies, there was always an Indian agent who was supposed to help the Indians, but, as it turned out, he was the one who had been selling them whiskey and guns? That's what the preacher you found to marry me looks like. A crooked Indian agent."

91

"Quiet, Running Mouth," said Ludlow. "The service is about to begin."

My bride was gorgeous. I wore a double-knit suit and had long sideburns. It was 1973.

I knew we were in trouble when the minister opened his Bible and began the service by announcing, "It says here . . ."

He lost his place several times and Ludlow's wife, the maid of honor, had to take his Bible away and find the appropriate spot so that he could continue.

After much stopping and starting again, after a number of eye-rolls I gave to Ludlow, my best man, for locating this refugee from Sermonette, the ceremony ended.

"Here are your train tickets," Ludlow said. "Your train leaves Savannah this morning at two o'clock and you'll be in Fort Lauderdale by ten."

There are no trains from Atlanta directly to Florida. You have to go to Savannah for that. I put my new bride in my blue Grand Prix (with white upholstery) and we headed for the Georgia coast.

I must make a note at this point that my stepbrother, Ludlow, is an accomplished practical joker. But it never occurred to me that he would try anything cute to cause a problem for me in my newly acquired wedded bliss.

The second Mrs. Grizzard and I arrived at the Savannah train station at approximately one A.M., an hour early for the train. The waiting room was filled with various coughers and throat-clearers and one man who blew his nose every thirty seconds. Coughers and throat-clearers are one thing. A nose-blower is something else altogether. Always avoid nose-blowers on trains and while sitting at a counter in a restaurant eating soup.

"Don't worry, sweetheart," I said to my wife. "Ludlow has arranged a deluxe bedroom for us."

I went to the man at the ticket counter. I told him who I was and that I wanted to confirm my deluxe bedroom on the two o'clock train to Fort Lauderdale.

"First," he said, "the two o'clock's running two hours late. Second, you don't have a deluxe bedroom. You've got two roomettes."

"Roomettes," for the rail-impaired, are tiny little things with a single bed that folds down out of the wall. There is barely room for one person in a roomette. Two people might get into a roomette. Whether they could get out again without the use of heavy equipment and blow torches is another question.

"Surely, you are kidding," I said to the ticket agent. "You don't understand. I just got married and this is my honeymoon night."

I also mentioned Barbara Stanwyck, Harry Truman, and Casey Jones, but it didn't do any good.

"You have roomette two," he said to me, "and the lady has roomette six."

My bride took it better than I did.

"We'll have our honeymoon night tomorrow at the hotel," she said.

"You don't understand," I said back, mentioning again Barbara Stanwyck, Harry Truman and Casey Jones.

That was probably the first time she ever had doubts about our marriage.

Just then it hit me.

"Ludlow did this," I said.

"Did what?" my wife asked.

"He got us separate roomettes as a joke."

"He wouldn't do anything like that on your wedding day."

"He would have put sugar in Lindbergh's gas tank," I said.

We had two more hours to kill in the station, so I called Ludlow and awakened him.

"That's really funny what you did," I said to him.

"What's that?" he asked.

"Getting us separate roomettes," I went on.

"You think that's funny?" said Ludlow. "Let me tell you something else. You know that guy who married you? He was no preacher. He runs the Texaco station down at the corner."

I never told my wife any of that, even as we were divorcing three years later. I always figured if a ship's captain could marry you, so could the Man Who Wears the Star.

The train finally arrived. Somewhere, highballing it down Florida's east coast, my wife and I managed to find a way in her roomette. The next day, I had various bruises and a nosebleed. She had a crick in her neck and later married her chiropractor.

Learning from my first two honeymoon experiences, I suggested to my third wife we not even leave town for our wedding night.

We took the bridal suite at an Atlanta hotel.

It was located on the basement floor of the hotel.

The lamps had been bolted on their stands so they couldn't be stolen.

The Jacuzzi was stopped up.

A friend of mine dropped by and we watched a basketball game on television.

That caused a fight when my friend left, and my bride threw her wedding ring at me.

Georgia lost the basketball game.

If I ever get married again, I'm going to suggest separate honeymoons.

My third wife and I, during our four-year marriage, did wind up doing a lot of traveling together. As a matter of fact, she accompanied me on my first trip to Europe, where sex is an important part in most people's lives, too.

Diplomats and heads of state do not travel in the style we did. My wife, who later married a man named Schmook and moved to Montana, made all of the arrangements.

We traveled first class, ate at the best restaurants, and the Gucci store in Florence later added a wing to the building as a result of our visit there.

We were away for three weeks. The first leg was a flight from Atlanta to Frankfurt. It took approximately eight hours. Do you know how much "free" booze you can drink on a flight between Atlanta and Frankfurt? When the flight landed, and I took my very first step onto European soil, it wouldn't hold me up.

"I cannot believe that I am in Europe with somebody who drank so much on the plane he can't stand up," my wife said to me, as I attempted to bring myself to an erect position once more.

"It's these blue boots," I said. They had given us blue booties to wear on the plane. I had forgotten to take mine off and put my shoes back on. My wife went back to the plane and got my shoes. When she returned, I had returned to a standing position, with the help of a chair.

I put on my shoes and then I asked my wife, "What should I do with my blue boots?"

"Why don't you take those blue boots and shove 'em right up your . . ." She didn't finish for fear there might be a fellow Junior Leaguer somewhere in hearing range.

After we got our bags—we were to transfer to the railroad station for a rail trip to Venice—I wanted to go to the sex shop.

"What sex shop?" my wife asked.

"I read about it in the *New York Times,*" I explained. "Germans are very liberal when it comes to sex, and they have a sex shop right here in the airport."

"What do they have in sex shops?"

"Maybe French ticklers and that cream they advertise in dirty magazines that will make your penis larger."

"Let's hurry," said my wife.

"I'm not going in there," she said when we found the sex shop.

"They don't have Junior Leaguers in Germany," I said. (I was always giving my wife hell about the Junior Leaguers. My favorite Junior League line is, Why do Junior Leaguers hate group sex? All those thank-you notes.)

"You don't know who might be in there," my wife replied. "You go in and see if they've got any of that cream. I'll wait out here."

They didn't have any of the cream, but they had everything else, including giant dildos of every size, shape and color, even an orange one that was so big, it was difficult to lift.

I decided to play a very funny trick on my wife. I took the big, orange dildo outside the store and hollered to my wife, "Is this the one you were talking about, honey?"

I figured there would be enough people around who spoke English to appreciate the hilarity of my remark.

"No," she replied, "but be sure to buy extra penis-enlarger cream. For you, one jar won't make much difference."

Clever, my third wife, who later would write a book about me and title it, *How to Tame a Wild Bore*. Never again will I marry a literate woman.

I returned the orange dildo and we caught a cab to the Frankfurt train station. There were a few hours until the train left, so I decided since I was in Germany, I would drink some German beer.

I even learned my first German words that morning: *"Ein Bier, por favor."* I also was hungry, so I perused the menu in the station restaurant.

I'd never eaten much German food because they put sauerkraut all over everything, and I hate sauerkraut. Probably the reason Germany keeps trying to take over the world is so they won't have to eat any more sauerkraut. Somebody should have thought to ask Hitler about that.

I had no idea what anything was on the menu, so I decided to roll the dice. I ordered something that seemed fairly easy to pronounce.

What it turned out to be was a giant wiener and a round, hard roll. Being still somewhat intoxicated at the time, I thought what I had in front of me was the German version of the hot dog, and I tried vainly to find a way to put the long wienie in the round roll.

Finally, I knocked the roll off my plate, and being hard and round, it began to roll out of the restaurant. I was behind it in hot pursuit.

The thing rolled all the way out on one of the platforms and a man smoking a pipe tripped over it and fell. I didn't want to get involved in any sort of lawsuit on my first day in Europe, so I went back inside the restaurant to eat the wienie.

When I got back to my table, however, my wienie was missing.

I tried to make the waiter understand.

"Somebody took my wienie," I said.

The waiter said something in German I didn't understand. At this point, my wife, who had been straightening out our tickets, joined me at the table.

"What's the trouble?" she asked.

"I lost my wienie," I said.

"When did you see it last?"

"It was here on my plate when I went to chase my roll."

"You were chasing a roll?"

"Yeah, it fell on the floor and rolled out onto one of the platforms and a man smoking a pipe tripped over it. I don't think he was hurt. Anyway, when I got back my wienie was gone, and I'm starving."

"I'll order you something," she said, and proceeded to name one of the selections. I was impressed.

"You know how to order in German."

"I've been here before, remember?"

I had another *"ein Bier"* or two before the waiter brought my food back. It tasted a little funny, but I was starving.

"By the way," I asked, "what was that I just ate?"

"Pig brains in milk gravy," my wife said. "They're a delicacy in Germany."

I never did find out if she was telling me the truth, but I went to the rest room and threw up just to be on the safe side.

I slept through most of the train trip to Venice. I had a horrible nightmare in which I was attacked by ferocious pigs wearing orange dildos around their necks.

Later, at the Gucci store in Florence, my wife bought a pair of Gucci boots and I purchased a pair of brown Gucci loafers for myself. I also wanted to buy a Gucci leather riding crop.

I knew all about riding crops because there was a pictorial in *Penthouse* magazine that showed two lovely, naked girls cavorting with a man in a Nazi outfit. In the last picture, one of the girls had put on the Nazi's black boots and hat, and he was naked. (I don't know what happened to the other naked girl. Out looking for a long wienie and a round roll, perhaps.)

The girl who remained was holding a riding crop and was lashing the Nazi with it. ("Giving him a sexy taste of her crop" is what it said under the picture.)

I thought I might give my wife a taste of my crop every time she complained about something.

"I'm cold."

Wap!

"When is this game going to be over?"

Wap!

"What do you mean, coming home so late?"

Wap!

"Put that riding crop back," my wife said before we left the Gucci store.

"I won't," I said.

She grabbed the crop from my hand.

Wap!

I put the riding crop back.

I've traveled all over the world since then and rate Amsterdam as the sexiest city I've ever been to. They can display sexy magazines in storefront windows, and when Jerry Falwell gets wind of that, there's going to be trouble.

The Greek isles are a terribly romantic place, too,

especially after a night of eating squid and octopus. If you think oysters can do the trick, try a little squid and octopi.

I even went to the South of France once and hung out on a beach where females were sunbathing topless. That wasn't as sexy as it would seem, however. The problem was the only females who were topless were those twelve and under and sixty-five and over. Travel agents should tell you about that before you go ahead and spend all that money to get to the South of France.

The least sexy place I've ever been was the Soviet Union. I was somewhat surprised when the Marines guarding the U.S. Embassy in Moscow got involved in the sex-for-secrets scandal with Soviet prostitutes.

Frankly, I didn't see very many Soviet women who were attractive or had thin ankles. I suppose if I had been a young Marine far away from home and some Natasha without thick ankles promised me sex, Commie-style, I might have given away a secret or two, also, but nothing harmful to our national security.

I'd have said, "Get out of the market by October nineteenth or take the Broncos and give the points. Elway's arm is one hundred percent."

I later heard of a private American citizen who had sex with a Soviet citizen.

He was from the South and he was visiting in Moscow in connection with an agricultural exposition. As he sipped a cocktail in his hotel bar one evening, he was confronted by a lovely Soviet woman.

The man bought the lady a few drinks and then they went to his room.

"She said she was a direct descendant of Catherine the Great and wanted five hundred.

" 'You Americans,' she said. 'You are all so rich. You can afford, no?'

"That's what I said, 'no.' I told her I was just a country boy from the South. I had been doing some figuring in my checkbook earlier in the day and it was lying on my nightstand.

"The princess spotted it and said, 'But, look. You have all these traveler's checks. You pay me with that.'

"So I picked up a check, wrote her one for five hundred, handed it to her and said, 'Princess, you're now 'bout to go 'round the world.' "

CHAPTER FIVE

It may be a weirdo thing to do and indicate your mother was frightened by a duck while she was carrying you, but have you ever given serious thought as to the love lives of certain animals?

How, for instance, do elephants do it? Or giraffes? The duck-billed platypus? The hummingbird?

Where is Marlin Perkins to answer these questions? He probably was finally eaten by a giant anaconda, which is what he deserves.

Remember watching Marlin on Mutual of Omaha's *Wild Kingdom*? All Marlin did was talk about the animals. It was his assistant, poor Jim, who had to do the dirty work.

"Here we are in deepest, darkest Africa," Marlin, dressed as Stewart Granger, would begin.

"Today, our subject is the ferocious lion. Jim, I'll hold the camera while you go inside the lion's den and see if any of the jungle's monarchs are at home.

"That's right, Jim. Get your butt inside the den or you'll be back cleaning out the monkey cages at the Omaha Zoo where I found you.

"Look, there goes Jim into the den where he greets the not-so-friendly lioness protecting her cubs. Sorry, Jim. She took that arm off clean as a whistle, didn't she?"

One of the ways to learn about animals' mating habits, rather than by watching Marlin and Jim (who now answers to the name of "Lefty") is to watch public television.

Most public television is a terrible waste of money. All you ever see is some boring British story involving somebody named Reginald who's always going around saying, "You cahn't do that, Sidney, you just cahn't."

Plus, you have to sit through all that time when some four-eyes is begging you to send in money to keep public broadcasting on the air. At least when Jimmy Swaggart or Jim Bakker begged for money, they put a little show biz into the thing. They at least cried or whined about having to pay off their bills.

All you get on PBS is, "If you become a member at

the forty-dollar level, we'll send you a valuable premium, such as an album featuring Peruvians playing the flute or a certificate indicating you have adopted a whale."

(It has occurred to me that if we continue putting forth efforts to save the whales, one of these days we're going to be up to our eyeballs in whales and I'll bet those things smell terrible.)

Occasionally, however, there is something worth watching on PBS. Recently, I watched a program entitled *Great Moments in Nature*.

I learned a great deal about animals' sex lives watching that program. For instance:

—Abalone don't even touch when they go through the reproduction process. The girl abalone releases about six million eggs into the water, and the boy abalone does the same with his fertilizer. If the currents happen to put some egg and fertilizer together, then there are more abalone. This is called "broadcast reproduction," which also can be seen on the Playboy Channel most any night.

—There are some birds—I forget what kind—who select their mates by dancing together. The birds dance around with this bird and then that bird until they have matched up with one whom they consider to be their best partner. After that, they go out in the parking lot and have wild sex.

These birds are the exact reason Baptists won't make love standing up. They are afraid somebody will think they are dancing.

—Male sheep who live in certain parts of the Holy Land and are mentioned in the Bible indicate to a female sheep they would like to mess around by sticking out their tongues at them. The human equivalent to that is saying, "What's your sign?"

—Some forms of animal life even have both reproductive organs and can reproduce without any outside help, which brings up a thought a friend of mine had once:

"If gay people can't reproduce," he asked, "why are there so many more of them than there used to be?"

The animal I know most about is the dog, because I have owned several of them over the years. When I was seven, I had a dog named Duke Snider. I named him after my favorite baseball player, the Dodger outfielder.

One day, Duke Snider had six puppies. All male. I named them Pee Wee Reese, Carl Furillo, Junior Gilliam, Gil Hodges, Johnny Podres, and Joe Adcock, some of my other favorite Dodgers.

When I was eight, my cousin came to visit me. He was older and his parents had been square with him about the entire sex thing. When I introduced him to Duke and the puppies he said, "Don't you know anything? Joe Adcock plays for the Braves."

I later learned about the reproductive habits of dogs firsthand. I inherited a basset hound named Plato while I was in college. Plato was a gorgeous red-and-white male who once ate my first wife's panty hose. I should have known then he was a little strange.

After I was out of college and ready to raise a family, I decided to mate Plato with a friend's female basset, Patsy.

I took Plato over to my friend's house. I thought I would leave him there a few days, some magic would take place, and Plato and Patsy would bring forth some baby bassets.

"You have to help me mate them," my friend said once I was at his house with Plato.

"Whatever do you mean?" I asked.

"The female basset," he explained, "has a weak back and cannot support the male when he mounts her. I will support Patsy. You hold Plato so he puts as little weight on Patsy as possible."

I was very confused by this.

"How long have basset hounds been around?" I asked.

"I'm not sure," he said.

"A long time, though," I said.

"I would assume so, yes. Why?"

"What I want to know," I answered, getting to the point, "is if today's female basset hound can't have puppies unless somebody holds the male and keeps his

111

weight off her, what did basset hounds do, say, two hundred years ago when maybe they were just out in the woods together and got the urge and there was nobody around to do any holding?"

"You want to mate these dogs, or not?" my friend asked. I made a mental note to write the American Kennel Club about all this, but, sadly, I never got around to it.

Neither did Plato and Patsy. When we put the two dogs in the same room together—my friend's basement —Plato knew there was something strange and marvelous happening to him.

He barked as only a basset can bark: "Bah-rooo! Bah-roooo!"

And he sniffed around on the floor, wagged his tail and had that look about him that said, "I'm not sure what this is all about, but I think I'm really going to like it."

Patsy, meanwhile, was being quite coy about the entire situation. As Plato drew nearer and nearer to her, she seemed to sense his stirrings and braced for his arrival.

(I was quite embarrassed myself. I tried to take a clinical approach to the matter, but I couldn't help feeling like I was an intruder.)

Finally, as if some instinctive voice or force charged Plato to grab for the prize nature provide him, he made his move.

Patsy fell flat from his weight.

"Hold him up off her!" shouted my friend.

Patsy stood up, most ladylike, and readied for Plato's next charge.

Up he came.

I grabbed for his chest to hold his weight back.

He jumped back, snarled at me and ran to the corner of the room and sat down.

"Let's leave them in the room alone for awhile," said my friend. "I think Plato is just a little nervous."

An hour later, we tried again. As soon as I would reach for Plato, in my most fervent effort to aid him, he would snap, dismount and head for the corner.

"I think," I said, "Plato wants to do this on his own."

"But he can't," said my friend.

"Bah-rooooo!" bellowed Plato, as if to disagree vehemently.

Patsy, meanwhile, had gone into an itching and scratching fit on the other side of the room.

"Your dog has a real attitude problem," said my friend.

I almost mentioned the panty hose incident, but I thought better of it. Something like that could go on a dog's permanent record.

My friend and I finally ended our little argument and decided the best thing to do would be to leave Plato at his house for a few days.

"Perhaps," he said, "they will find a way."

But they never did. Some few days later, Plato, obviously homesick, and tired of his *objet d'amour* ate a pair of my friend's $175 Gucci shoes and he made me come and get my dog.

As far as I know (I soon lost Plato in a divorce settlement, which is another long story that I have covered in a previous effort), Plato never fathered any puppies, but did once attempt to force himself upon an unsuspecting Shetland pony.

All that got him was a kick upside the head. Plato, as my ex-wife explained to me in her message of Plato's death (at fourteen), gave up on sex after that and took to howling mournfully at the moon and spending an inordinate amount of time with a neighbor's cat named Sissy Boy. I will take any conclusions I derived from that to my own grave.

It would later come to pass that I would know another dog who devoted his life to lovemaking, however. He belongs to two of my very best friends, Dee and Jimmy Matthews of Albany, Georgia.

The dog's name is Deuce. He is a black Lab. People who know Deuce often say, "If there is such a thing as reincarnation, I want to come back as a dog and I want to be exactly like Deuce."

Deuce sleeps at the foot of Dee and Jimmy's bed. When Deuce wants a dog biscuit, he goes to the closet where the dog biscuits are stored and gives one loud bark. Dee promptly fetches Deuce a dog biscuit.

When Deuce wants to go outside, he goes to the door and barks. Dee promptly opens the door. When Deuce is outside and wants to come back in, again he barks, again Dee rushes to the door.

"We'll never know how many puppies Deuce has fathered," Jimmy Matthews has said. "But it's a considerable number I am certain."

Albany, Georgia, is a fairly large town.

"Deuce has girlfriends in every portion of the city," Jimmy further explains, "not to mention several others in Sasser and Dawson."

A man in Albany raises pit bulls, which are known for their vicious, aggressive behavior. One of his pit bulls went into heat. One afternoon, Deuce came calling.

He leaped over a small fence in which the pit bull was being kept and proceeded to have his way with her. The pit bull owner saw what was happening, and attempted to run Deuce away before anything of any consequence took place.

Just to be certain he had turned away Deuce in time, he took his pit bull to a vet and had any possibility of his dog's subsequent pregnancy stopped.

He also went to the hardware store, bought more fence and wire and constructed what witnesses indicated was a barrier six feet tall in order to make certain there was not another incident such as the one that involved Deuce.

Several days later, however, our hero returned to the home of the pit bull, scaled the fence with ease and satisfied his desires for a second time. Jimmy Matthews tells the rest:

"When the pit bull turned up pregnant, the owner knew Deuce had been at it again. He called and was quite upset. He also mentioned he worked for the IRS, which got my attention.

"I calmed him down, though, and suggested the union between a black Lab and a pit bull might prove interesting."

The pit bull gave birth to seven puppies. They turned out to be calm, loving dogs with great leaping abilities. The girl dogs got their father's hot blood and were known to hang out in bars and talk to sailors. The boy dogs chased poodles with pink ribbons and all got tattoos that said, "Born to Raise Hell."

I said to my friend Jimmy Matthews, "Shouldn't you have Deuce fixed? There are so many unwanted dogs as it is."

"I know that," he answered. "But I just can't bring myself to do that to ol' Deuce. Besides, he's got a reputation to uphold."

I'm a horse racing fan. Nothing in sport is quite as exciting as the moment the gate opens and all that tonnage of horseflesh bursts away with my financial future dependent upon which horse is in the biggest hurry.

A horse racing joke:

There's this fellow who hangs out at the horse track a great deal. One evening after he has gone to sleep, his wife is cleaning out the pockets of his pants before putting them in the washer.

She finds a note inside one of the pockets with the name "Shirley" and a phone number. The following morning, she confronts her husband.

"Who is Shirley," she asks, "and what about this phone number?"

"Shirley is a filly I bet on at the track yesterday. The phone number belongs to my bookie."

The next afternoon, the man arrives home again. He asks his wife, "Did I get any mail today?"

"No," she replies, "but your horse called twice."

My favorite horse racing event is the Kentucky Derby. Louisville on the first Saturday in May is like Augusta National on the last day of the Masters golf tournament, New Year's Day at the Rose Bowl, Mardi Gras in New Orleans, and Saturday night at the Possum and Sweet Potatoes Festival in Dump Truck, Alabama.

Everybody dresses up, drinks a lot of whiskey, and spends a lot of money.

As much as I enjoy Derby Day, however, something I saw prior to a Derby several years ago still causes my amazement, as well as my concern.

I went to an actual horse breeding. What I mean to say here is I was in the stable when they brought in a mare and then went and got a stallion and right there, as a lot of people looked on, they did what horses do.

Again, as in the case of basset hounds, I caught myself wondering, how did horses reproduce when there was nobody around to take care of the details? There were a good six or seven people involved in this thing.

I will start at the beginning.

I was a guest for lunch at one of the horse farms in Lexington, two days before the Saturday running of the Derby. I can't tell you exactly which farm it was, but it's not far from where Phyllis George lives and my hosts were laughing about this mutt of a dog that hung around the horse farm and went over to Phyllis's house and messed with her two poodles or some such dogs.

(Maybe they were poodles, but I forget exactly what kind of dogs they were, but it seems to me Phyllis George is the kind of person who would have poodles, with names like Pierre and Fifi.)

I told everybody about Deuce and the pit bulls and then I thought to myself I'd never known just how interesting and humorous the sex lives of animals could be.

But back to the horses. We were inside the stallion bar. A huge door opened and a man led in a horse.

"Here's the mare," somebody said.

"Does something like this cost a lot of money?" I asked.

"Stud fees are enormous," I was told.

Some papers were signed and the man who led in the mare did a lot of talking to the man who was identified to me as the stallion master. I expected a stallion master to look like Charles Bronson. This stallion master looked like Roddy McDowell, but that has nothing to do with this story and I don't know why I even brought it up.

When all the talking and signing ended, the mare was led over to the side of a stall which had a small window in it that was covered by a wooden door.

"What's going to happen now?" I asked.

"They're taking the mare to the teaser," it was explained.

What happened next was the door was removed from the window of the stall and a horse—I have no idea of his name—stuck its head out the window, because that's all he could get out of the window, and began chewing on the mare's neck.

"What happens here," I was told, "is the teaser bites the mare's neck, which is sexual foreplay for horses. After the teaser has finished getting the mare ready, the stallion will be brought in."

I didn't say anything right away. I had to think the entire thing through first.

The mare comes in and somebody leads her over to the window in the stall. The window is opened and a horse sticks its neck out and bites the mare on hers.

This excites the mare. Then, they close the window on the teaser and then the stallion comes in to finish the job.

"But," I asked, "does the teaser also get, well, aroused?"

"I suppose so" was the answer.

I suppose so. What sort of dirty deal is this and does the SPCA know about it?

The poor teaser sticks his neck out, gets the mare ready to rumba and then gets the window slammed in his face.

He does all the dirty work and all the stallion has to do is show up on time.

"Does anybody ever concern themselves about the teaser?" I also wanted to know.

"What do you mean?" said my guide.

"Well, it's got to be terribly frustrating to be asked to arouse mares all day and then never get the satisfaction of being able to follow through. Isn't he provided a lover of his own occasionally, just to keep him from going insane?"

"That would seem to be a sensible thing to do," I was told.

"Not to mention humane," I said.

Anyway, now the window has been closed on the teaser, who doesn't even get to watch, and out come two guys leading the stallion, who somebody explained won the Florida Derby and placed in the Belmont.

He is led over to one corner of the room, while the mare is taken to an opposite corner.

"They're going to prep the stallion now," said the man calling the play-by-play.

I'm not going into exact details of what all prepping a stallion involves, but I wouldn't want the job because I would be afraid I would be at a nice dinner party somewhere and somebody would ask me, "What do you do?"

"I'm a stallion master, ma'am."

"How intriguing. Just what does that entail?"

"I prep the stallions."

"Go on."

"Well, I get the stallion ready to perform."

"Perform what?"

"Well, you know . . ."

"No, I'm afraid I don't."

Then, I would try to explain the teaser and that would be even more confusing and I'd finally leave the room in complete embarrassment.

It doesn't take horses long. The stallion is led over to the mare. Two guys hold on to him when he locks himself into position.

Then the mare is led away and put back in her van and the stallion is sent back to his stall.

"Who knows," somebody said. "Perhaps we have just witnessed the start of another Secretariat."

Still, I couldn't get my mind off the teaser. We're spending all this money and attention on saving the whales and here's a poor horse who's got to be on the edge of a nervous breakdown.

Before I left the stallion barn, I walked over to the teaser's stall and opened the window. The teaser stuck his head out. I scratched him on his head and patted him on his neck.

"Hang in there, pal," I said.

Later in the evening after a few beverages, I said to my female companion, "I think I know what I want to come back as if there's anything such as reincarnation."

"What?"

"A teaser in a stallion barn."

"Why don't we go on to bed, sweetheart, maybe I can take your mind off it."

"Not tonight," I said. "It would hardly seem fair."

CHAPTER SIX

If I could have sex with any movie star I pleased, I'd pick Kim Basinger. I thought she was wonderful in *No Mercy* with Richard Gere, especially when they were wandering around in the Louisiana bayou country and Kim got her outfit wet.

She was best, however, in the movie *9½ Weeks*. I never did actually figure out the plot to that movie, but I didn't really need one to keep my interest. Likely, Mickey Rourke, the costar, didn't need one either.

Mickey Rourke did some strange stuff to Kim Basinger in that movie. Some of his moves likely would have astounded Dr. Ruth and been an entire chapter in the next Hite Report.

What I never can figure out about movies with sex scenes in them is: How do the actors and actresses figure out a way to look passionate for the scene, but yet remain unattached enough not to have to be pried apart by the dolly grip after the scene is over?

I'm not certain I could do that, especially if I were in a steamy scene with Kim Basinger. They'd have to hose me down with cold water or beat me with large sticks in order to get my attention.

The movie *9½ Weeks* had a lot to say about the sexuality of food. Recall that Mickey Rourke enjoyed covering Kim Basinger with certain foods—I seem to recall strawberries—and then feasted on them, not to mention Kim.

This caused me to have my own food fantasy about Kim Basinger.

I'd think you'd have to really take your time figuring out just what foods were important if you were going to put them on Kim Basinger.

This is not a woman who would wear something like pork and beans that well. For pork and beans, you need ZaSu Pitts.

I would tend to think in terms of foods like mayonnaise, Kool Whip, Mrs. Butterworth's syrup or Oregon Farms carrot cake.

I'd put food like that on Kim Basinger, then have my way with her and then we'd shower to get the Mrs.

Butterworth's out of our hair. After that, my life would be complete and I would spend the rest of my days writing her love sonnets and convincing her to fill our pool with Jell-O and frolic naked through it. She didn't even do that with Mickey Rourke.

I think Kim Basinger's emergence on the screen has signaled a return of sex symbols to movies.

There were a lot of movie sex symbols when I was growing up. Besides Marilyn, there was Jayne Mansfield, Diana Dors, and Mamie Van Doren, who later married Bo Belinsky, whose career as a major league pitcher was over shortly after.

Even the so-called legitimate actresses had their moments. Dorothy Malone used to knock my socks off. Then there was Gina Lollobrigida in those biblical movies.

What parents of my generation never knew was that movies based on Bible stories showed more actual skin than such movies as *A Summer Place,* where Troy Donahue did it with Sandra Dee.

Gina Lollobrigida did the Dance of the Seven Veils in some long-forgotten Bible movie and I, quite frankly, was nothing more than a walking pillar of salt for days.

Then we went through a period of movie actresses who were smart, could learn all their lines and actually could act. The problem was most of these women had very little sex appeal, and with certain exceptions such

127

as *Kansas City Bomber* and *The Guns of Hattie Calder* with Raquel Welch, movies became quite heavy and void of any sort of good, old-fashioned lust and passion.

Diane Keaton became a big female star, for instance. Diane Keaton may be a great actress and was perfect in *Reds*, but she has a smart mouth and she isn't the least bit sexy.

And neither is Meryl Streep, for that matter, and I am always having to defend myself when I write that Meryl Streep, albeit a great actress, is a dog.

I couldn't for the life of me figure out why Robert Redford, who could have had any woman inside the jungle or out, wanted to waste so much time on Meryl Streep in *Out of Africa*.

And then Robert DeNiro flipped over her in that movie where he was an engineer and she had a husband out in Connecticut somewhere and, believe it or not, Jack Nicholson marries her in *Heartburn*, which I thought was a terrible movie.

In the first place, all Meryl Streep did was whine in that movie. In the second place, I would have gotten my fill of that and run around on her too.

I think we're mostly over that sort of movie, however, and we're back to some steamy sex coming out of Hollywood:

Here are my favorite sex scenes out of some recent movies, in no particular order. I ate not one morsel of popcorn through any of these:

—Mickey and Kim and the strawberry.

—Kathleen Turner and William Hurt in the tub in *Body Heat*.

—Mickey Rourke and Lisa Bonet in *Angel Heart*.

—The two kids in the bus on *Planes, Trains and Automobiles*.

—Dennis Quaid and what's her name in *The Big Easy*.

—The "El" scene with the hooker and Tom Cruise in *Risky Business*.

—Debra Winger on the mechanical bull in *Urban Cowboy*.

—Debra Winger and Richard Gere cavorting in *An Officer and a Gentleman*.

—The girl washing the car in *Cool Hand Luke*. I know this isn't a recent movie, but it came to mind, so I just threw it in for old times' sake.

—Glenn Close and Michael Douglas in the elevator in *Fatal Attraction*.

This movie struck chords in most everybody. As I mentioned in Chapter 1, in this time of sex that will kill, here was something else to worry about. What if *you* had a weekend fling and it turned into the nightmare of *Fatal Attraction?*

"I'm going to see that movie," a man said to me, "as soon as I decide who to take with me, my wife or my girlfriend."

Of course there is also the X-rated genre of movies to discuss in any exercise regarding sex and films. (The reason I said "films" is so I would appear to be somewhat of a sophisticate. People who said "film" instead of "movie" usually attended a school without a good football team and didn't think Joe Don Baker did a helluva job in the classic, *Walking Tall.*)

The first X-rated movie I saw was in a trailer park, *Tillie Goes to the Dentist for a Filling and a Drilling.* The experience taught me an important lesson in watching nekkid movies.

It really should be very dark where they are showing stuff like that. The primary reason is, if a bunch of your buddies are around, if you spend an overly large amount of time staring at the screen, they'll laugh at you. This causes a certain uneasiness in the viewer.

X-rated movie houses realize this, of course, and now the darkest place you can go to that is still above ground is to an X-rated movie house.

Before going any further there should be at least a brief discussion concerning adult theaters themselves.

It takes a lot of courage to go in one of those places. First, God knows who might see you going in. Stand right there at the ticket window and buy a ticket to see

Thar She Blows, which actually was an X-rated movie, and you know what is going to happen.

A bus is going to stop at the corner. Inside the bus will be your mother, your minister, your former scoutmaster, high school football coach and shop teacher, not to mention everybody in your Rotary Club, Willingham, the office gossip over in shipping, and Jerry Falwell.

Say what you will say, but it won't do you any good.

"I was just getting some change for a pack of cigarettes when you pulled up, and . . ." you will whine feebly.

But your mother will know exactly what you're up to.

"After all I've done for you," she will say, "this is the thanks I get."

"Don't worry about it, Henrietta," your family minister will say to your mother. "We all know he wasn't raised this way."

"I knew," your scoutmaster will chime in, "there was something weird about you, boy, when you couldn't tie a bowline hitch."

"The little sumbitch is a pervert, that's what he is," will be your former high school football coach's thought.

"You got that right, Harvey," your shop teacher, the one who had three fingers missing from his right hand

and flunked you on "Using Your Power Saw Safely," will add.

Willingham, meanwhile, will have it all over the office by the next morning that you were spotted going to see a skin flick, the fellow Rotary Club members will make you program chairman for eleven straight years, and Jerry Falwell will shout, "Kill him, for he is a *fornicator!*"

If you really want to go into an X-rated theater, go at night and wear a hat pulled down over your eyes.

Some other points:

—Don't eat the popcorn in an adult theater. You simply never know where that popcorn has been.

—Move very slowly once you are inside the theater and are attempting to find a seat. Because of the darkness of the theater, God knows what, or whom, you could mistakenly sit upon.

—Don't become vocal no matter how exciting or explicit the screen action becomes. "Hot damn, would you look at that!" shouted in an X-rated movie house is about as attractive as shouting, "Where'd you get that weird hat?" when you have an audience with the pope.

—Never doze off in an X-rated movie theater. You could be taken advantage of in various ways that come to mind.

—As you leave the theater, make certain there are no buses out front, and then run to the next corner and pretend you were just out to get a paper.

I'm not going to deny that I have been to a few X-rated movie theaters. I saw *The Devil in Miss Jones* and I saw *Deep Throat* in X-rated theaters.

I also went to an X-rated movie theater in New York City. It is only now, many years later, that I can talk about the experience.

There were three of us in New York. There was Norman, Rainey and me. Rainey had never been north of Knoxville, Tennessee. He didn't want to see the Statue of Liberty. He wanted to see a dirty movie.

We looked in the paper and there was a movie entitled *Behind the Green Door*, starring Marilyn Chambers, who used to be on the cover of a box of soap when she was a baby, but that was a long time ago and Marilyn has changed a lot since back then.

The three of us paid five dollars each and Rainey wanted some popcorn.

I explained to him why that was not a good idea.

We walked into the theater and the movie hadn't started yet and it was like walking into an endless abyss.

Rainey kept walking on the backs of my shoes.

I am leading my two friends and I am feeling my way into a seat. It was like putting my hand into dark water, hoping a snake or an alligator didn't bite it off.

Suddenly, I touched something hairy.

"Good God!" I tried to whisper.

I jerked my hand back and then began to feel around again. I found a pair of ears, which made me feel a lot better.

"It's somebody's head," I said to my two companions.

"I'm very sorry," I said in the direction of the head I had felt.

"I was just trying to find a seat."

The head didn't answer. New Yorkers.

The three of us climbed over what was attached to the neck of the head and took our seats.

When the movie came on the screen, I looked and noticed we had climbed over an old man who was asleep.

Here was the plot of *Behind the Green Door:* Marilyn Chambers is taken prisoner and a large black man performs unspeakable acts to her person for about an hour and a half.

When he finishes, a cast of a thousand get involved and there's a trapeze involved and the old man sitting at the end of the row hadn't stirred. This began to disturb me.

The movie continued and it was difficult to see who had hold of what and Marilyn Chambers had to have just about given out by then, but she continued attempting to please what had grown to be a rather large contingent of men, all at the same time.

Suddenly, I see a flashlight coming down the aisle. It is the theater's usher. He shines it into the old man's face and says something that sounds like, "Okay, pops, outta heah."

Again, the old man doesn't stir.

"You don't leave, I'm callin' the cops," says the usher.

Not so much as a twitch of an eyelid. This is becoming much more interesting than the movie. Even Marilyn Chambers' repertoire of sexual moves had run out and she had begun repeating herself.

"There's something strange going on here," I say to Norman and Rainey. Rainey's mouth is still halfway open, indicating absolute dumbfoundedness at what he is witnessing on the screen.

Five minutes later, two policemen come in. They have flashlights, too.

"Harry," says one officer, "would you look at that on the screen, Harry?"

Harry makes a guttural response. I think he's in love.

They shake the old man again. Still, no movement. They do this perhaps three more times and Harry says, "What we got here is a stiff."

What I am saying here is that the three of us were in New York City in an X-rated movie house watching

Marilyn Chambers have sex with enough men to start a Rotary Club and we're sitting next to a cool one.

Rainey, meanwhile, is still watching the screen and has no idea what is happening at the end of our row.

"Don't tell Rainey," I said to Norman. "He's about to have a stroke just watching the movie."

Soon, two guys roll in a stretcher, put the old man on it and wheel him away.

"What's wrong with him?" Rainey asked.

"See what happens when you eat the popcorn in a place like this," I said.

That was my last trip to an X-rated theater, and I don't see how those places stay in business anymore. If you want to see some sex on the screen, you need look no further than your own television.

You can subscribe to the Playboy Channel, for one. They don't actually show entry on the Playboy Channel, but that's about all they don't show, and after watching those nature films on PBS, I'd just as soon not see the actual linkage, if you know what I mean, and I am certain you do.

If you really want to see the hard-core stuff, you can simply order yourself a bunch of X-rated tapes and put them on your VCR and watch them in your own living room and eat safe popcorn.

A friend of mine subscribed to one of those movie rental places where you call, and they actually deliver the tapes to your house.

"I told my wife she needed to be a bit more kinky," my friend said, "and she wanted to know if that meant she had to dress up like a chicken or be tied to anything."

"I said, 'No, honey. Why don't we watch a few X-rated movies together?'

" 'You call the tape rental,' she said, 'and I'll start the popcorn.'

"So I get out the rental catalog and look down the list of X-rated movies. I decide to order *Talk Dirty to Me* and *Dirty Talking*.

" 'I'm sorry,' said the guy on the phone at the rental place. 'We're out of *Talk Dirty to Me,* the original, but we have *Talk Dirty to Me II.*'

" 'I'll take that,' I said.

" 'We also don't have *Dirty Talking* in right now, either. How about *Talking Dirty?*'

"I ask, 'That's not the same movie?'

"The guy says, 'No. *Dirty Talking* is one movie and *Talking Dirty* is another, although you might find some similarities between the two. As a matter of fact, the same furniture shows up in both movies.'

" 'Okay,' I said. 'Then give me *Talk Dirty to Me II* and *Talking Dirty.* I hung up the phone and my wife brought in the popcorn. 'You nibble on this,' she said, 'and I'll go change into something more fitting the occasion, speaking of nibbling.'

" 'This is really going to be some night,' I'm thinking,

when the phone rings. It's Doofus back at the tape rental place.

" 'Are you the guy who ordered *Talk Dirty to Me II* and *Talking Dirty?*' I say I am.

" 'Well, I'm very sorry,' this guy goes on, 'but *Talking Dirty II* is missing and it turns out we do have *Dirty Talking* and not *Talking Dirty.*'

" 'Look,' I said. 'Just send me over a couple of movies where people take their clothes off and have sex. I don't care about the titles. I don't care about the actors or actresses. Can you handle that?'

"The guy says, 'That's fine.' My wife comes down in a sexy negligee, cuddles next to me and finally the movies arrive. They brought *Naughty Stewardess IV* and *The Gland Hotel.*

"I put one in the VCR and mashed all the buttons and nothing happens. All I've got on my screen is a bunch of lines and no sound.

"I keep trying with no success. I unplug all the wires on my TV and plug them into other holes. Nothing.

"My wife, meanwhile, is falling out of the mood, and so am I. We finally gave up on the movies and called Domino's for a pizza. I said no anchovies. They brought anchovies. I went to bed.

"The next morning, I come down for breakfast, and my eight-year-old kid has been fooling around with the VCR and is watching a two-on-one fast break involving two naked stewardesses and the idiot who's supposed to be flying the plane.

"'What are you watching?' I said to my kid.

"'A *ménage à trois*,' said my kid, 'but you probably don't know what that is.'

"'When did you learn to speak Spanish?' I asked him. My kid just laughs at me and heads for school. By this time, the stewardesses are working on the navigator.

"I took both the tapes back to the store on my way to work and picked up *Mr. Smith Goes to Washington* with Jimmy Stewart and *Three Came Home* with Claudette Colbert, which I watched in my undershorts while drinking a six-pack.

"My wife took a look at me and said, 'What a difference twenty-four hours makes, Johnny Wadd.' What did she mean by that?"

His wife, I explained, was referring to Johnny "Wadd" Holmes, the pornographic film star/lover whose business was measured, as mentioned in an earlier story, from the floor. I also informed him we were speaking of the *late* Mr. Holmes.

"The popcorn?" my friend asked.

"I'm not certain," I said.

Johnny Wadd Holmes died in 1988 at age forty-three.

In an interview prior to his death (which sounds sort

of stupid, since he couldn't have been interviewed *after* his death), Holmes claimed he had had sex with 14,000 women.

This is a staggering claim and may indicate that the cause of his demise was something other than popcorn.

Think about 14,000 women. That's more women than are in a lot of towns and small cities. Paducah, Kentucky; Gorham, New Hampshire; Pooler, Georgia; Wedowee, Alabama; Stanley, Idaho; and Casper, Wyoming, come to mind. Can you imagine having sex with every woman in Paducah, Kentucky?

I put the pencil to the 14,000 women thing. Here's what came out:

Let's say, just for argument's sake, that Johnny Holmes became sexually active when he was fifteen. That means his sexual career lasted twenty-eight years. I multiplied 28 times 365 and came out with 10,060. So, Johnny Holmes had 10,060 days to have sex with 14,000 women. That's about 1.4 per day.

Now certainly he took days off occasionally. I mean there must have been days when he was ill, and there just had to be days when he said, "Listen, I just want to sit here in my shorts and drink beer. Call me back tomorrow."

What all this means, I concluded, is that Johnny Wadd Holmes had some days he had no sex at all, which means there were days he had an amazing amount. There must have been days he had sex with at least a dozen women.

Further questions should be asked:

—On these multiple days, did he achieve an orgasm each time?

—Did his partners?

—How long a break did he take in between activities?

—How long did he have to talk to each of his sexual partners after they had finished having sex?

—Did he smoke after each sexual act?

—Did he maybe die of lung cancer?

—Could he name each of the fourteen thousand women?

There was also some speculation that Johnny Holmes died of AIDS. That might be, of course, but I think some thought might also be given to the possibility that his heart just gave out before his most photographed part.

Sex for audience entertainment goes back to caveman times when a group of the guys would sit around and watch their friend Nork bash his woman over the head with a club. There are the rumored donkey acts in Mexico and you can go even today in Times Square where theaters advertise live sex acts on stage.

I first became interested in sex as a spectator sport when my boyhood friend and idol, Weyman C. Wannamaker, Jr., a great American, brought a deck of dirty playing cards to school. His cousin, who was in the navy, had given them to Weyman. Each card pictured a man and a woman involved in a sexual act. Their faces were covered with those black bars they used before somebody figured out nobody was looking at the faces.

Weyman rented the cards to his schoolmates. They were a nickel for one recess period. He got a dime if you wanted to keep one through lunch. For a quarter, you could take one home with you. I paid a quarter, took home the three of spades and studied it with great intensity. The position of the two individuals in the photograph appeared to be in defiance of gravity, as well as many other laws of nature.

When I turned my card back in to Weyman, at precisely 8:30 the next morning to avoid a late charge, I asked, "Do you really think it can be done like this?"

Weyman was around my entire boyhood to explain such questions to me.

"This is the way they do it in France," he said.

The French are quite a supple lot, I thought, and made a mental note to visit that country at some point in the future.

Sometime later—when I was thirteen—there came the marvelous opportunity actually to see women with very few clothes on. The county fair, held each fall, had a new attraction that year, known in the parlance of the day as a hoochie-coochie show.

Word got around quickly of this marvel.

"The work of Satan!" was the Baptist preacher's critique.

"They don't wear anything over their boobs," said Weyman, who was not an actual eyewitness to this phenomenon, but had heard two men talking about it after church Sunday.

Weyman and I went to the fair together. We walked directly past the cotton candy, didn't even pause to pick up a few ducks for prizes, ignored the guy guessing weights and went straight to the hoochie-coochie show.

I was nervous. I didn't know if we would be able to get in at our age.

Four women were on a stage outside a tent. They were all wearing suggestive outfits. One was wearing mesh stockings. There was a tear in them. A crowd of men had gathered to look at the women. An announcer had joined them on stage.

"Shirley here," he said, pointing to the girl with the

143

rip in her hose, "is famous for her 'Airplane' dance. I can't tell you much about it boys, but you ought to see her tail spin."

Laughter. I didn't understand the joke.

The announcer continued down the line, introducing each girl.

There was Suwannee. "You've heard that song, boys. 'Way down upon Suwannee . . .' More laughter I didn't understand. Suwannee was a sad-looking woman, perhaps in her early thirties, who had fat ankles and a bruise on her right leg. She chewed gum as she was being introduced.

Then, there was Brown Sugar, a black girl whose lips were painted a ferocious red.

"You know what they say, boys," said the announcer. "The blacker the berry, the sweeter the juice."

More laughter. I was pretty sure I understood that one.

Next was Beverly. "She's got some hills you're not going to believe," the announcer went on. That I not only understood, but also was mildly amused by.

It cost a quarter to get inside.

"You like what you see on the outside, you're gonna love what you see inside," said the barker.

"How old you got to be to get in?" I wondered to Weyman.

Just then the announcer said, "Come on in, anybody, all ages. Just remember, if you're eighteen you won't understand it, and if you're eighty, you might not be able to take it."

Weyman and I paid our quarters. I had a total of fifty cents to spend at the fair. That would leave me with enough for one ride on the Ferris wheel, a couple of trips on the Scrambler and a Coke. It would be a night to remember, I told myself.

There were maybe fifty men—and two boys—inside the tent. We sat on drink crates. Some of the men opened up fruit jars and guzzled whiskey.

None of the four women got totally naked. I probably couldn't have stood that. I was moved enough when Beverly, who wore pasties on her hills, did this amazing thing where she swung one of them around in one direction and then got the other going in the opposite.

"Don't that beat all," said Weyman.

Suwannee came out and lipsynched "Way Down Upon, etc." with Al Jolson, which is rather difficult to bump and grind to, I would imagine, but Suwannee, ever the showwoman, pulled it off, so to speak.

Brown Sugar's dance number was "Camptown Races." She seemed to "do" when she needed to "dah," however, and I got the feeling this entire situation bored her.

Shirley closed the show. She came out wearing an aviator's cap and mostly wiggled her butt to a rather scratchy recording of "Those Daring Young Men on the Flying Trapeze."

When the show was over, we all stood and gave the dancers a standing ovation.

Somehow I knew that after seeing that show, cotton candy, the Ferris wheel and watching baseball games with my grandfather would never hold the same thrills they once had.

But the old county fair strip shows and dimly lit joints where strippers hustled their champagne cocktails at twenty dollars each are mostly a thing of the past.

What took their places were nude dancing parlors. I'm not certain who first had the idea to start a nude dancing parlor, but the idea brought a completely new era to taking one's clothes off in public.

The first time I was ever in such a place was in Memphis in a club near the airport. I walked in, ordered a beer and looked around me. Nude dancers were everywhere. I was Linda Blair in *The Exorcist* trying to see everything at once.

These were not fat women with bruises and tears in their stockings. These were lovely young girls in remarkable physical condition.

The only time I had ever seen anything remotely like this was at my tennis club where they offered aerobic exercise classes.

After tennis, it was customary to stop by and look into one of the exercise classes. At some point—I know not why or when—the baggy sweatsuit had been replaced by tight, revealing exercise outfits.

When the ladies jumped around doing their drills, everything jumped around with them in a rather pleasing way.

My mind often wandered back to the county fair and the girl with the this-a-way, that-a-way breasts as I watched the aerobics class.

Watching women do stretching exercises in their little outfits is rather interesting, too, because of the refreshing angles you get. So bumping and grinding had become an exercise. It used to get you arrested.

Back to Memphis. I learned a new phrase that evening. It was the "table dance." In Memphis, the girls said table *daintz*.

What you got for five dollars and any tip you wanted to hand-place in the dancer's garter was she would stand on your table and dance a song for you, completely butt nekkid.

I had myself a table daintz and enjoyed it, except for one thing that made me a little uncomfortable.

Understand that I was sitting down at my table and this vision of loveliness was standing on my table. As she danced, she looked down at me. When I looked up at her, there was something that caught my eye on the way up.

Was I supposed to look at her in her eyes, which you

could get for free? Or was I supposed to look elsewhere and indicate my shameless interest in what I was shamelessly interested in?

I sort of divided my time looking both at her face and at what she moved with a rhythm that was quite fetching indeed.

I've had some interesting things happen to me in such places. I have never made it a habit to hang out in nude dancing parlors, but you get to one now and then for bachelor parties, and to celebrate such things as Arizona getting statehood, Grover Cleveland's birthday, Thursday, and making it another day without getting a kidney stone.

Once, in a place called Solid Gold in Fort Lauderdale, I actually met a nude dancer who was quite famous. She had been picked as Miss Nude America on the Playboy Channel.

I paid her for three table dances and then asked her to marry me. I offered her my watch, my ring, my red Chevy Blazer and season tickets to University of Georgia football games.

She declined.

"I'm having too much fun entertainin'," she said, "to go off and get married."

I could see she, indeed, enjoyed her work. When she left my table, a group of sailors came in and when I left, she was on her fifty-seventh table dance for them.

Her name, by the way, was Fonda Love.

"My agent is real clever," she had explained to me.

At this writing, the nude dancing parlors in Atlanta, where I live, are still open. Atlanta is famous for its nude dancing parlors.

When the city was awarded the 1988 Democratic Convention, the *Wall Street Journal* did a piece profiling the city. The article was divided into four major themes: Atlanta's hotels, its cabs, its barbecue and its "internationally acclaimed nude dancing clubs."

Despite this, however, and despite the fact that the clubs are clean, the girls make enough money on tips and the club makes enough money on drinks that nobody has to hustle customers. The state legislature even passed a bill in the winter making it unlawful to sell alcohol where people are dancing without their clothes on.

Georgia's governor, Joe Frank Harris (his personality and vision go with his name) signed the bill into law.

Perhaps someone will think of a way to put a halt to this madness. If not, there will still be nudie clubs, but the low-rent hustle will be back in place.

That hurt my feelings. At this time, I am waging an all-out effort to keep our beloved nude dancing halls. Perhaps an appeal can overturn the law or maybe somebody will pay off the right people at the state capital and the nude dancers can dance on.

At any rate, those of us who want to see the clubs saved even have a slogan. For years, citizens battled to save Atlanta's historic Fox Theatre. They were successful.

One of Atlanta's most popular nude dancing spots is the Cheetah III. Our slogan: "Forget the Fox. Save the Cheetah!"

There also is the constant battle to keep ourselves safe from censorship when it comes to various publications.

I first came across such censorship also at a young age—the dreaded scissors taken to my school's *National Geographics*.

Most of us turned to the Sears, Roebuck catalog for our thrills after that. There usually were pages and pages of women models in some sort of underwear in each edition. Just to be sure, I asked Weyman one day, "It's just the underwear you can order, right? Not the women, themselves."

He assured me I was correct. I expected that response, but I wanted to make absolutely certain.

By the time I was in high school, *Playboy* was flourishing. I will never forget the first copy of *Playboy* I ever saw. There was a picture spread of Jayne Mansfield, including shots of Jayne in the bathtub with only a bubble here and a bubble there to cover her.

What made *Playboy* so successful at its outset, I think now, is Hugh Hefner knew men who bought the magazine often would be confronted by various females such as their mothers, girlfriends and wives with such comments as, "I can't believe you spend money on trash such as that."

What Hefner had done, of course, was to fill in around the pictures with some high-sounding articles written by high-sounding writers so a man, so confronted, could issue one of the great lies of all time:

"I don't buy *Playboy* for the pictures. There is some great reading in here."

Some men may have said that so much they came to believe it. Not me. I've glanced at the *Playboy* Interview a few times over the years and once even read an entire article because it was written by somebody I knew.

I usually do look at all the cartoons, of course, and think the best one I ever saw was of a small boy, obviously David, swirling his slingshot around his head as he stood next to two large feet, which obviously belonged to Goliath.

The caption showed Little David saying, ". . . And if he gives me any jive, I'll take him in five."

When I lived in Chicago for a short period, I even dated a girl who worked for *Playboy*. As a secretary.

I had to find out, so I asked her:

"You know the captions with the pictures of the girls where they are saying things like, 'Art makes me so passionate' and 'I like a man who can share my love of classical music'? Do those girls really say things like that, or does somebody write it for them?"

"Those bimbos?" the girl answered. "Their brains are in their bras."

So they aren't Phi Beta Kappas, I thought to myself. As long as they knew a couple of state capitals and could make at least an occasional complete sentence, I would be satisfied.

Playboy is now much more risqué than it once was. Frontal nudity and all that sort of thing.

I suppose *Playboy* simply had to keep up. *Penthouse* took the next step in magazines with sexual themes. It left nothing to the imagination in its nude pictorials, as well as the letters readers allegedly sent in to be published.

I can't find out for certain, but I'm almost positive somebody at *Penthouse* makes up those letters. I'm forty-two years old and nothing has ever happened to me like what happens to those people who are supposed to be writing them. I don't even *know* anybody who's had such experiences.

Some guy is always picking up some college beauty queen in a bar and going home with her only to find her two voluptuous roommates are there and the four do things to one another that may be impossible to do with the restraints the human body puts on itself, and I don't think everybody in those letters is French.

The reason I'm suspicious about *Penthouse*'s letters is I sent them one of my own and it was never printed in the magazine. Here was my letter:

I am an incredibly good-looking forty-year-old guy and I walked into a Baskin-Robbins ice cream place for a quick cone.

Behind the counter was an incredibly good-looking, tan young woman.

I ordered butter pecan and as I waited for the young woman to scoop it out for me, she began to disrobe.

She had an incredibly good-looking tan body. She motioned for me to come behind the counter.

Soon, I was completely nude, too, and she was putting butter pecan all over my incredibly good-looking tan body. Suddenly, the entire cheerleading squad from the University of Nebraska came into the store for ice cream.

All eleven of them took off their clothes, unveiling their incredibly good-looking tan bodies.

The thirteen of us took turns putting ice cream all over each other and I suffered frostbite on my incredibly large, tan nose. From that point on, whenever I eat ice cream, I feel the urge to take off all my clothes and sing the University of Nebraska fight song.

I've been arrested twice for it, and you'll never believe what happened when the young,

blond jailer with the incredibly beautiful tan
body walked into my cell and said . . . etc.

After continuing to read *Penthouse* letters after
sending in my own missive, I decided I hadn't involved
enough people in my episode. One letter I read told of
a man who had sex with the entire Junior League of
Omaha while yet another did it with nineteen female
mud wrestlers and the Albright Sisters, a Gospel En-
semble of Fructose, North Dakota.

I tried two more times. One letter described how I
had played strip canasta with the entire student body
at the all-girl Brenau College in Gainesville, Georgia,
and in another I was explicit in narrating my involve-
ment with the 400-strong Rent-a-Maid Co. in Okla-
homa City. I threw in a lot of stuff about mops and
furniture polish, but I got no results, so I stopped my
Penthouse letters campaign.

Beyond *Playboy* and *Penthouse,* of course, are the
real sleazo magazines like Larry Flynt's *Hustler,*
which is absolutely sick, perverted, stupid, unenter-
taining and worthless.

Hustler, of course, printed the satire on Rev. Falwell
indicating he had had sex with his mother. Falwell
sued. The case went all the way to the Supreme Court.

Who do you pull for in something like that? It's like
picking a favorite between cancer or heart attack, fat
or ugly, Iraq or Iran.

It took me about three seconds to decide who I was for:

Flynt.

Here's why:

Give the book burners one little victory like Falwell over Flynt and those people can get absolutely red-eyed with determination to see everything but the Bible, *Reader's Digest* and *Guns and Ammo* flushed down the toilet.

You've seen people like that. They have beady little eyes, the men wear knee-length socks and sandals with their bermuda shorts and eat a lot of prunes, and the women have moustaches and dowager's humps. They tend to speak partially through their noses.

They not only want to censor books and magazines, they would like to do away with anything that is fun, such as doing it with the lights on and drinking in the daytime.

These people have no sense of humor, keep plastic over their living room furniture, like Bob Barker, send money to television evangelists, buy velvet paintings of Jesus and/or bullfighters from people selling on the side of the road, drive ugly cars, don't like dogs, are pale, are still wearing polyester and haven't had a decent bowel movement in twenty years.

S. J. Perelman referred to such individuals as "damp people." I could add to that by saying they are the mushrooms of the human race.

Let them have a say in what we can read or watch or do and, pretty soon, the rest of us will be just as bored as they are.

As far as protecting children from seeing nudity in magazines or on television, the best thing to do is never mention it and they'll probably be more interested in playing soccer or listening to music that, when played backwards, is a satanic chant.

Mention to your children that all that filth is behind the counter at the 7-Eleven store and you don't want to catch them looking at it and they'll break their cute little necks getting to it.

The Supreme Court did, in fact, hold that Flynt was protected under the First Amendment so Falwell didn't win his suit. The Larry Flynts of the world come and they go and, if we would all ignore them, they would go away forever.

The Falwells and the damp people are much more dangerous. If we are to be extreme in our tolerance of what is written, photographed or put on film, then let it be to the liberal side. Or, put better perhaps, I want to be able to sit at this typewriter and write what I damn well please, which is what I have done and now I'm finished on that subject, except to pass along one anecdote:

Somebody shot Larry Flynt in front of the court-house in Lawrenceville, Georgia, in 1978. He was on trial for peddling smut. The person who shot him was never caught.

They rushed Flynt to the hospital where there first was a fight to save his life and then a fight to save him from a life of paralysis. They saved his life.

As the press and curious onlookers stood vigil near the emergency room awaiting news from Flynt's doctors, I heard two elderly ladies talking.

One said, "You know, I read in the paper where Larry Flynt said he'd found the Lord. Reckon that's true?"

Replied the other, "I ain't so sure he found Him before, but I'll bet he's lookin' hard for Him now."

CHAPTER SEVEN

What I always wanted to know about the Jimmy Swaggart scandal was this: Just what sort of things were going on inside that motel room where the wealthy televangelist was reported to have paid a hooker for "pornographic acts"?

I took this report, when it broke, to mean the Rev. Jimmy wasn't in there actually doing it to the hooker but had paid for something else that otherwise titilated him.

The imagination knows no bounds here. Did one of the two participants dress up like a chicken? Were electrical devices involved? Did Jimmy get nekkid? Was the hooker playing Kim Basinger to Jimmy's

Mickey Rourke? Were live animals used in any fashion? Did anybody anoint anybody with oil? Did the Lord talk to Jimmy during any of this:

THE LORD: "What are you doing in there, Jimmy?"

JIMMY: "We're not smoking, Lord."

THE LORD: "Okay."

When it comes to sex and religion—and the two have been bound strongly since all that biblical begatting was going on—I have many questions, such as the exact nature of Swaggart's admitted "sin against God."

Here's some other stuff I want to know:

Is the story about Eve getting Adam to eat the apple allegorical?

I simply can't see banishing people from the Garden of Eden for just eating an apple. What were Adam and Eve supposed to live on? Butterfly wings?

I could never get any of my Sunday school teachers to level with me, but I think what really occurred in the GOE was Eve put a couple of moves on Adam and he took her over behind some grape vines and they had at it after God had given them strict orders not to.

I think God knew if Adam and Eve started messing around, it could lead to, well, God knows what and, of course, it did.

Is it really a sin to lust in your heart?

A former President of the United States said he couldn't help doing it, and I think it's the same with most people.

When I was old enough to understand what lusting in my heart meant, Kathy Sue Loudermilk was old enough to start wearing tight sweaters to school. I lusted after her in my heart, my nose, my pancreas, all over.

I even did this as she sat across the room from me in Sunday school and later as she sat next to me during the preaching service. Do you know how hard it is not to do a little heart-lusting when you are this close to heaven itself?

I prayed over this a great deal.

"Lord," I would plead, "please don't let me lust in my heart over Kathy Sue."

I'd even try to think of Harry Truman and it wouldn't do any good. If the Lord hadn't meant for me to lust, I'd ask myself, why has all the blood drained out of my head and headed south?

I also wondered what deeply religious people like ministers did when they got the urge. Could they turn off a lustful feeling at its origin?

A story:

Three ministers, Baptist, Methodist and Presbyterian, worked and lived in the same small town. It happened that all three took their annual vacations at the same time. They decided to take a group trip.

They rented a Winnebago and headed for the beach. On the way, however, they were involved in a head-on collision with a truck hauling hogs. The ministers and their wives were killed. The hogs were unharmed.

St. Peter was waiting at the Pearly Gates.

"How may I help you?" he asked the Methodist minister, who was first in line.

"I just got killed in a horrible wreck," said the preacher, "and I'd like to get into heaven."

"I'm sure that's no problem," said St. Peter, "but we do have regulations and I must check the file on you to be certain you are eligible."

St. Peter punched a few keys on his computer, studied the screen for a moment and then said, "Preacher, I'm very sorry, but our files indicate you are guilty of a cardinal sin."

"What did I ever do?" asked the astonished minister.

"Our files say you lusted after alcohol," explained St. Peter. "You never actually drank any alcohol, but you lusted after it, and that's just as bad. It says here your lust for alcohol was so strong, you wouldn't get married until you met a woman named Sherry. Now, if you'll excuse me, there are others."

The Presbyterian minister was next. He went through the same ritual with St. Peter.

"I've got some bad news for you, too," St. Peter said. "According to your files, you lusted after money. You never had any money, but it says your lust for it was so great, you wouldn't marry until you met a woman named Penny. Dismissed."

The Baptist minister, third in the line, overheard all this and turned to his wife and said, "Fanny, you and me might as well leave."

And another question arises: If you're going to be in the same amount of trouble for merely lusting, why not go ahead and satisfy that lust? If you're going to hell anyway, why not enjoy the trip?

Is God going to hold it against me for relishing the fall of Jimmy Swaggart and Jim Bakker?

That's one of the questions I think I can answer, and the answer is, surely not.

Don't these bozos embarrass God? Jimmy Swaggart is up there shouting and crying and I even saw him get in the spirit once and dance on the stage. Think how much money Fred Astaire could have made if he'd gone into evangelism.

And Jim Bakker is towing around Tammy Faye, his wife, who is a walking can of Sherwin-Williams paint. God had to cringe every time those two stood before a camera and hit up the multitudes for cash.

In Bakker's case, however, at least we knew his lust-ette's name and we even were treated to an exact description of the flesh-sinning he did with Jessica Hahn, who later posed naked for *Playboy* for lots of money and said, "I am not a bimbo."

Tammy Faye, meanwhile, reacted to all this by saying, "Shopping is the way I ease my nerves."

I guess that Jim and Tammy rode their water slide for Jesus so long, they both became soggy in the head and that is what led to their downfall.

As for Swaggart, he's first cousin to Jerry Lee (the Killer) Lewis, who kicks over piano stools and married his thirteen-year-old cousin. His hot-bloodedness indicates heredity could have played at least some part in the scandal.

Also, I'm not certain why this is, but the pulpit does strange things to some people, not to mention their families.

Faith healer Brother Roy Dodd Hembree used to come to my hometown each summer with his tent and his two daughters, and there are some who later witnessed that they had not seen certain moves the Hembree daughters put on before or since.

They would stand behind Brother Roy Dodd, as he preached and healed, in their white sundresses, smiling down on the congregation. When Brother Roy Dodd asked for a "Glory!" they'd shout, "Hallelujah!" and put a couple of wiggles in it and the sight of it all was a blessing to behold.

A new Baptist minister moved into town once and his daughter, who was in my fifth-grade class, held sex education classes behind the stands at the baseball field every day during recess.

This made it quite difficult to pay attention in the

geography class that followed recess. I still don't know exactly where Tasmania is, but it didn't seem important then and it doesn't seem important now, compared to the knowledge I gained from the Baptist preacher's daughter.

Religion is a passion to some, of course, and perhaps that passion reaches such a pressurized state that it boils over into other parts of the psyche, particularly whatever part makes one want to fool around.

The passion the women felt when Elmer Gantry preached was the same passion they felt when his terrible swift sword pierced their fragility. Give me a minister, a little sex and throw some money around and I will give you immense passion and fury. This is from a Gannett News Service article out of Verona, Mississippi:

> When George Pritchard pulled a gun and started firing a few Sundays ago, right in front of the Morning Star Missionary Baptist Church, people were stunned.
>
> It was strange and upsetting enough that somebody would spray gunfire around a church congregation; even with all the bad feelings and controversy that had contaminated Morning Star in the preceding months, nobody had expected gunplay. But on

a day when the preacher planned to sermonize on how the church belongs to God, the violence was utterly confounding.

It was, after all, the first time the Reverend Pritchard had ever been angry enough to shoot up the place.

"I didn't have any intentions of doing what was done," the minister explains. "It just happened."

Just blowing off steam, you might say. He was reacting to the latest episode in a bitter struggle at the church, hinging on whether Pritchard is or is not fit to preach the gospel of the Lord. Dissident congregants had accused him of financial mismanagement, using church property for personal gain and preaching favorably about premarital sex. They'd even voted, in a meeting of disputed validity, to oust him.

After fussing with enemies for so long, even a clergyman needs a release—and there's no release quite like scattering a crowd with a fusilade.

"They were the instigators," Pritchard says, noting that even Jesus resorted to violence while clearing the temple of the money changers. "You wonder why He did that."

In a way, folks shouldn't be so surprised by

Pritchard's actions. While it's possibly unusual for a minister to be packing a rod on the sabbath, the fact is these were peculiar circumstances. How often does a preacher show up for Sunday meeting to find a line of angry congregants blocking his path into the church?

"They just put up a line, locked hands," says Willie Moore, the man who brought Pritchard into Morning Star and who leads the fight to put Pritchard out. "He tried to walk through the line, but he couldn't. So they told him he couldn't come in no more. 'Today is your last day. Go back home.'

"He said, 'Yes, I'll go back.' He stepped back and went for his gun. A deacon held his hand down. He fired three shots, in the ground. Wasn't for the deacon, two, three people'd be dead."

Pritchard, who had been on crutches with an ankle injury, then threw down his crutches and hobbled into the church, the crowd having been effectively dispersed. Once inside among his supporters, he began preaching as if nothing were amiss. Sheriff's deputies arrived in midservice, but chose not to arrest him immediately.

"They let him preach," Moore says with disgust. "They thought they were being respectful to the church, but on the other way of looking at it, letting a man preach what just shot at his members, I wouldn't call that respecting God's house. What do you think?"

The real question, of course, is what the community thinks. Not only does Pritchard face firearm charges that could land him in jail, there's an argument that suggests a controversial pastor doesn't exactly cement his authority by going publicly berserk. Fire not upon the congregation, the axiom goes, lest ye yourself be fired.

"It's a mess," says T. K. Moffett, Pritchard's lawyer. "These are nice folks. Our prayer and our hope are that this issue can be resolved and this church can go on."

For his part, Pritchard simply disputes the allegations of the Moore faction. It was he who saved the church from fiscal peril, the pastor maintains. As for premarital sex, he says (in his precise words), "Fornication is a sin."

It all comes down to a question of power, he says, "Power and control." To Pritchard's way of thinking, it is high time for Willie Moore to face facts and recognize where the power rightfully belongs. That, by the way, seems to be the congregation's way of thinking, as well.

In a vote of confidence the other Sunday, a month after the shooting, Pritchard won 81–54.

But back to Swaggart and Bakker. Many people asked, why did these men risk their lives and their fortunes on illicit flings?

Both men were pulling in millions. Both had power. They, themselves, were worshiped.

Ask that question and you must ask it of all men who have strayed, been caught and had to pay the price.

Gary Hart might very well have been elected president of the United States had it not been for Donna Rice and the monkey business on the *Monkey Business*.

So why risk it all?

Actress Olympia Dukakis, who played Cher's mother in the movie *Moonstruck,* discovered her husband (Vincent Gardinia) was fooling around on her, and she asked the timeless question, "Why isn't one woman enough for a man?"

She ultimately decided it is because men fear death. They sense age is depriving them of their manhood and they want to prove to themselves that sense is wrong. Jimmy Swaggart's cousin, the Killer, sang:

> He's thirty-nine and holding,
> Holding everything he can,

> From seventeen to twenty-five,
> Just to prove he still can.

There is also—and I think this is even more of an influence in a male's decision to stray—the thrill of the chase.

It's not waking up in the morning and finding a conquest lying next to you in your bed. Eternity is how long it takes you to gracefully convince her to leave after you've awakened.

It's what happened the night before. The sighting. The initial contact. The convincing. That's the chase and that's when the blood runs the hottest, the senses are most alive and why it's hard for a lot of men to give it up.

I had a friend who was getting married the day after we threw him a huge bachelor party. We had booze and we had music and, suddenly, my friend became visibly depressed and walked outside the party room.

I followed him.

"What's the matter?" I asked. "You getting nervous about all this?"

"My problem," he said, "is I've found what I'm looking for, but I'm not sure I'm through looking."

The marriage lasted less than a year.

Getting caught messing around in the wrong pew, as was the case of Messrs. Swaggart and Bakker, is really what this is all about, of course.

Swaggart got caught. Bakker got caught. Hart got caught. Most do, no matter how careful they are to cover up any of the evidence.

How a man handles himself when he is caught says a lot about him, I think. Warren Beatty was nailed for having flings with all those women in the movie *Shampoo*.

"Okay," he said to his lover. "I did it. I did it with all of them."

"But why?" she asks.

"I don't know," he answers. "It just sort of makes my day."

Swaggart and Bakker, of course, whined a lot and quoted Bible verse. Swaggart even went on television and said, tearfully, "Oh, Lord. I have sinned against you." A bit melodramatic for my taste.

Gary Hart blamed the entire thing on the news media and then had the audacity to get back into the presidential race. Probably because his wife had him on such a short rein, the only way he knew to get out of the house and meet girls again was to take his collapsing show on the road again.

I heard of a man once who was vacationing in Miami Beach with his wife. She went shopping and he went to the beach and met some lovely thing. They wound up back in his motel room. His wife wasn't due back for hours.

When his wife burst in and caught the man in the

173

act, he responded by saying, "Honey, I know it looks like me, but it's not me. I swear it's somebody else."

Nice try, but she took him for everything he had in the ensuing divorce action.

There are several schools of thought as to how a man should best handle the situation if he is, indeed, found out.

Women are fond of saying, "If you will just tell me the truth, there won't be a problem."

"You really mean that, honey?"

"Of course I do. As long as you don't lie to me I can handle it."

"Okay, then, the truth. I had sex with Arlene Finglehammer last Thursday afternoon at the Ramada Inn and it was fabulous."

"You rotten, sneaking, lying, no-account . . . etc."

It's better not to tell the truth. We all know that, of course, but we kid ourselves. The truth is no matter what they do to you, how much they beg you or how much they tell you they can forgive you, never admit anything.

"Yes, this is Arlene Finglehammer in bed with me, but there has been no entry, therefore no harm has been done."

Another rule to follow if, say, you are, in fact, caught in bed with Arlene Finglehammer and you are naked, is before you do or say anything, make certain you have your pants back on.

Never is a man as vulnerable as when his pants are off. You can't think straight, your credibility is at an all-time low and you can't even run away.

I knew a man who had been out all night playing around and snuck back into his house at six in the morning. As he was pulling his pants off to get in bed with his wife, she awakened and looked straight at him.

Quickly, he started pulling his pants back up to his waist.

"Big day today, honey," he said. "I've got to get to the office early."

I am by no means trying to condone adultery here, but the fact is, it's one of the most popular of the Ten Commandments to break. Who goes around making graven images today?

And may I say one other thing: If you do decide to stray, you'll eventually get caught.

There have been many instances of men going a little crazy when they discover their women have been cheating on them. Gurney Potts back home found out his wife was clandestinely cavorting with Farley Knowles, a renowned sheetrocker.

The first thing Gurney did was beat Farley Knowles within an inch of his life, and then he took his wife to the court square in town and while hundreds of interested bystanders looked on, he gave her a severe paddling, using an oar he had sawed off for more effectiveness.

This may seem somewhat cruel, but remember we at least don't brand women with scarlet letters anymore and the dunking pool has been obsolete since the last witch left Salem.

I think women are more creative than men when it comes to getting their men back for being unfaithful to them.

For instance:

One woman is credited with finding out her husband is seeing another and she follows him to the other woman's house.

While he's inside, she calls for a cement truck and has her husband's Mercedes convertible filled with cement.

Women also can express their displeasure at infidelity with violence. While researching this effort, I asked many of my friends and acquaintances who had been caught cheating to tell me how their wives handled the situation. What follows is a few of their stories:

RAUNCH BOTTS, free-lance gynecologist: "I was sitting in my favorite bar with a bimbo I had met earlier in the evening.

"We're getting along quite well, and I figured I'm in like Flynn when I see my wife walk in the front door.

"I looked for a place to hide but she already had

spotted me. When she got to the table and began to scream at me, I pretended to go nuts.

"I began babbling incoherently and drooling. Somebody said, 'He's speaking in tongues!' Somebody else said, 'No he isn't. His eyes aren't rolling back in his head.'

"I began rolling my eyes back in my head.

"Then I ran from table to table knocking over people's drinks and then tried to eat one of the large ferns in front of the bar. I then went into a corner, curled up in the fetal position and whimpered.

"The bimbo I was with ran out screaming and my wife grabbed a bar rag and began flailing at me with it.

"The manager called the cops and they hauled me away and took me to a nearby hospital for observation. A psychiatrist came in the next day and gave me the Rorschach ink-blot test. I identified one blot as my mother refusing to breastfeed me and another as my father dressing in my mother's clothes.

"The psychiatrist called my wife and told her I needed complete peace and quiet and that I could not be held responsible for any of my actions. She bought it.

"Unfortunately she caught me roller-skating in the nude with a dental hygienist two weeks later and pushed me down a steep embankment. It was two months before they took all the stitches out."

DUDLEY BLECH, Ginsu knife salesman, whose wife followed him to a motel where he met his mistress, one of the counter girls at the Dunkin' Donuts:

"It was awful. Me and Sheila was just opening the first page to *Penthouse* Forum to get in the mood and maybe get a few new ideas about tying one another up or using ice cubes when my wife starts banging on the door, yelling, 'Dudley Blech, you so-and-so, I'm gonna kill you and that hussy you're with. Now get out here! I've got a gun!'

"Then she fired a couple of rounds through the door, but neither me or Sheila was hurt. I had to think fast. I opened the door and my wife stormed in waving her piece.

"I said, 'Stop, honey, it's not what you think. This poor woman isn't my lover and nothing is going on here you should be mad about.'

" 'Well,' said my wife, 'if she's not your lover, who the hell is she?'

"I knew she would ask that, but I was still stalling for time. Finally, I said, 'This poor woman is my sister we thought was lost when the tornado hit our trailer back in '49.

" 'When the wind quit, we looked all over for little Sheila here, who was just four years old at the time, but we never did find her. We just figured the Lord had decided it was time to call her home.

" 'But would you believe it? She tracked me down,

her favorite brother, and called me and said to meet her here. I thought it was somebody pulling a thoughtless prank, until I got here and found out my blessed sister was alive and well.

" 'Sheila, I want you to meet my wife, Doris Fay.'

"I thought I had it made, but suddenly Doris Fay spotted the *Penthouse* Forum and the rope Sheila had brought. Sheila got away clean, but I was winged in the left shoulder. They charged Doris Fay with disturbing the peace, assault with a deadly weapon and biting one of the arresting officers.

"By the time she got out of jail, she wasn't nearly as mad as she had been. All she did was knee me in the groin a couple of times, put out one of my eyes and shoot my dog. After that, she pretty much forgot about Sheila. I guess that's what attracted me to Doris Fay in the first place. She's always been so forgiving."

Despite what has been discussed to this point, I do think monogamy may be the way to go in the future.

First, there is the fear of AIDS. As great as sex is, it isn't worth dying for. It's worth getting hurt a little for, spending a lot of money for, and going to a lot of trouble for, but it's not worth dying for. Even if you never have sex in your life again, at least there's eating, golf and gin rummy left.

Secondly, there's the *Fatal Attraction* angle, which

can get you killed, too. Maybe even by a straight razor.

Thirdly, there's the crackdown on drunken drivers. Nobody has really discussed this effort and its relationship to sex.

I would think that a very high percentage of illicit sex rendezvous involves alcoholic beverages. I mean, very few people score at the Christian Science reading room or at a Taco Bell.

They meet at bars or at parties and the more they drink, the more invisible they become and, pretty soon, they're out the door in a frenzied search for privacy.

They're serious about DWI's in this country now. They will put you in jail and take a great deal of money if you get caught driving while drinking. The fear of a DWI has somewhat immobilized the pickup bar crowd. I have a friend who was stopped following a young lady home at two in the morning after meeting her at a bar.

He was taken to the police station and put in the tank.

"I was wearing a pink Ralph Lauren polo shirt," he said. "The only other people in the cell are these two giant black guys.

"I go to one side of the cell and sit by myself. One of the black guys walks over to me and says, 'Can I have your breakfast?'

"I said, 'You certainly may.' I was in there for three hours before a friend got me out. All the time, I was thinking, 'Nobody is good enough in bed to have to go through this.' "

The alternative to drinking booze in a pickup bar, of course, is to order something like Perrier.

The problem there is I would be afraid to go home or have sex with anybody who would pay $3.50 for a glass of water with a lemon in it.

The basic point here is that, for at least a while, monogamy is going to be in style and you'd better make the best of it, which means both partners are going to have to work at keeping their sex life entertaining and interesting.

"Strange"—the male term for sex with somebody you probably shouldn't be having sex with—will be replaced with what you're used to, despite the tattered phrase that has been a part of male sexual beliefs for years: "Having sex with your wife is like striking out the pitcher."

That, of course, is not necessarily the truth if you have a wife who will, in fact, get a little kinky occasionally. A husband who will also use his imagination and will cater to some of his wife's needs can also help a monogamous relationship be quite an exciting one.

Even Cordie Mae Poovey, a girl from school who was uglier than a train wreck and twice the size of one, and her husband, Hog Philpott, mechanic and bird-dog raiser, have had a wonderful sex life throughout their entire marriage. In fact, pound for pound, Cordie Mae and Hog may be as hot a couple as there is.

I wanted other couples to be able to learn Cordie Mae's and Hog's secrets to a successful monogamous relationship, so I asked them each to share what they have learned during their many years of marriage.

Cordie Mae wanted to go first.

"It's the little things I do for Hog that keeps him out of beer joints and back at the trailer with me at night.

"I always try to look my best for him when he comes home from the service station or back from training his dogs to point at birds, or whatever those good-for-nothing hounds do besides just about eat us out of house and home and bark all night so the neighbors can't sleep.

"Larcy Threadgill who lives two trailers down woke us up at two in the morning screaming about Hog's dogs.

" 'Make them dogs shut up, or I'm callin' the pound in the morning and have every damn one of 'em put to sleep.'

"Hog said to her, 'Why don't you git back to your trailer and do something about them brats you're raisin'? My dogs are a lot better behaved than your children and twice as smart, too.'

"She went and got her husband, Grover, who came over and said he was going to whip Hog's butt. Hog said, 'You goin' do what?' and Grover said, one more time, he was going to whip Hog's butt.

"Hog's butt weighs twice what all of Grover Thread-gill weighs, and so Hog let him have one upside the ear. Grover allowed as how he'd make his wife shut up about Hog's fine bird dogs.

"When we got back to bed, I told Hog what a manly thing he had done and how much I enjoyed watching him thump Grover Threadgill, and one thing led to another and pretty soon we had that double-wide just about rockin' off the blocks it sits on.

"But back to always trying to look my best for Hog, I shave my legs twice a month, whether they need it or not, and I go down to the Kurl 'n' Kut and Bonami Wharton (they named her after that cleaning powder) teases my hair up.

"One time, Hog came home right after I'd been at the Kurl 'n' Kut and he said, 'Cordie Mae, I believe Bonami's done teased your hair to the point it's taken offense.' Hog always did have a good sense of humor.

"I also try to dress for my man. I thought Hog would like me in a pair of tight jeans.

"How I squeezed into them things I'll never know, but when Hog saw me in them, he went wild. 'Course, it didn't do him any good because by the time I found my pinking shears and cut my way out of them over-alls, Hog's mood had done passed.

"What else turns Hog on is my perfume, Wild Hare. One sniff of that and he's all over me. His dogs don't like it, though. If I go out to the pen with it on, they start howling and scratchin' in the ground.

"I think the most important thing in keeping a man interested, though, is being willing to go along when he wants to do something you either never heard of or was done back in the days of the Romans when they wore those robes without any underwear on beneath.

"If Hog says he wants to make love to me in the living room with the lights on with *Entertainment Tonight* on television, I don't argue. Hog even wanted to tie me up one time, but they didn't have enough rope down at the hardware store.

"What really drives Hog wild, though, is when I put some of my rasslin' holds on him. I was a professional rassler until they banned me for pulling a knife on a referee one night in Dothan. I'd spray myself with black paint and put on a mask when I went into the ring. I was known as 'The Masked Eggplant.'

"Hog likes for me to dress up like that and sling him around the trailer a little bit. One time, I went a little overboard and slung Hog right out the door. He must have rolled for five minutes. He come back all scratched up and bleedin' and say, 'Honey, I think I'll go to bed. That's all the lovin' I can stand for one night.'

"I think me and Hog will always be happy together and neither one of us will ever need anybody else. Besides, Hog knows if I were to catch him with another woman, I'd take him by the hair of the head and snatch him bald.

"All that dressin' in tight jeans will keep a man home ninety percent of the time, but if you want to make sure you can count on that other ten, then put the fear of God in him. Ain't no man can fool around with two broke legs and a hole in his face where his teeth used to be."

I thanked Cordie Mae for her guidance in this matter and then sought out Hog's assistance. How, I asked him as he was putting a new fan belt on a Buick, does he keep a smile on Cordie Mae's face?

"Women," he began, "like a man who's strong and willing to stand up for her. That dang Grover Threadgill over at the trailer park woke me up at two in the morning saying what he was going to do to my bird dogs—I got four, Rattler, King, Ernest and Sonny Boy, he's my favorite—and I let him hold Number One right in his mouth and I was about to let go Number Two when he commenced to apologizing and sayin' Sonny Boy was sure to win the county field trials the next week.

"I tried to get back to sleep after that was over, but Cordie Mae couldn't keep her hands off me. I thought we was going to turn over the trailer. Cordie Mae is a full-sized woman and when she gets passionate, you're on the ride and you can't stop and get off.

"I always try to compliment Cordie Mae on her looks, too, and I think that will keep a woman from lettin' herself go or erodin' on you.

"She goes down to the beauty parlor and gets her hair fixed and I always tell her how good it looks, except for the time Bonami Wharton—she's the one that does hair at the beauty parlor—sent Cordie Mae home lookin' like something that could scare a dog off a gut wagon.

"I said, 'Honey, I believe Bonami has done pulled a mean trick on you. I've seen better lookin' hair on fatback.

"Cordie Mae marched right back to the Kurl 'n' Kut and put out one or two of Bonami's lights and got that hair back to where it wouldn't make nothin' run away.

"I like to use my imagination in our lovemaking. One time we were listening to the radio and Conway come on and started singin' that 'Tiger in These Tight-Fittin' Jeans.'

"I said, Cordie Mae, why don't you get some of those jeans and we'll show Conway who's a tiger and who ain't.

"Bless her heart, she tried. She came home in a pair of Dee Cee overalls that had been painted on her. We wound up having to cut her out of 'em and by the time we finished I was wore out.

"Cordie Mae also likes for me to wear her favorite cologne, Sweat Gland.

"She says it reminds her of when she was a rassler. Cordie Mae was a professional rassler until she tried to cut a referee in Dothan one night after he disqualified her for laying out the first two rows of fans for calling her Shamu.

"The first time I saw Cordie Mae rassle, I said to myself, 'She's the one for me,' and I still get excited when she puts on her old rasslin' outfit.

"We were foolin' around there in the trailer, and I had Cordie Mae put on her tights. Well, one thing led to another and the next thing I know, she's slingin' me around over her head. I said, 'Let go, Honey, I can't wait no longer.'

"She let go, all right. I went right out the door and didn't stop rolling until I was three trailers down. Everything on me was bleedin' except my hair. When I came to, I said, 'Sweetheart, I believe I'm through for the night.' That sweet thing understood, of course.

"I always try to be willing to do whatever it is that is exciting to my woman and won't cause me to lose a lot of time at work.

"Cordie Mae likes to go off in the woods sometimes and mess around. Long as you don't mind a few briars, it ain't that bad.

"Cordie Mae also likes to fool around with the lights on in front of the television. 'Course, when she's on top, it's plumb dark for me and I can't hear the television anyway.

"One night, I said, 'Baby, let's pretend I'm the Marcus of Sod and I'll tie you up. I read a lot, is how I know who Marcus was.

"Cordie Mae said that would be fine, so I went down to the hardware store to get some rope and all they had left was a few feet. You start tyin' up a woman the size of Cordie Mae, you better have enough to lasso an elephant.

"What keeps Cordie Mae and me happy is we listen to one another, we try to take care of each other's needs and there just ain't no time or room for anybody else.

"Of course, I wouldn't fool around on Cordie Mae. I got mashed potatoes and hot gravy at home. Why would I go out lookin' for cold collards somewhere else?

"Besides, if Cordie May caught me with another woman, bein' slung out the door of the trailer would be mild compared to what she'd do then. That woman would flat cloud up and rain on me.

"So I guess I'll be a one-woman man until the day I die. See if it'll crank now, Carl," Hog shouted to the customer.

So, there's a profile of a devoted, monogamous 1980s couple. Let us review some of what we may have learned from them. To keep a lasting sexual relationship, it's important to:

—Be aware of your partner's needs and desires. Call the hardware store a couple of weeks before you'll need the rope to make sure they've got plenty on hand.

—Nothing is really too kinky. Unless it entails being thrown through the door of a trailer.

—Be certain to wear his favorite perfume and her favorite cologne. I'm not certain where you would find Wild Hare perfume or Sweat Gland cologne, but start by looking at your local K mart.

—If your partner is the size of a Winnebago and wants to get on top during lovemaking, learn to hold your breath for long periods of time.

—If you are a man and plan to fool around, never marry anybody who is capable of whipping half the city of Dothan, Alabama.

—Monogamy isn't all that bad, once you're used to it. It's safe, it's simple and you don't have to remember all those names.

CHAPTER EIGHT

I'm not certain the exact age that the male body and its parts begin to deteriorate. All I know is that I am now safely into my forties and although my mind is still capable of writing certain checks, my body can no longer cash all of them.

I've still got my hair, though, and that is a comfort. Friends who have lost or are losing theirs seem devastated by it. In fact, I had a friend who got married just because he had started losing his hair.

"I figure I'm completely bald in two or three more years," he explained. "So how many girls are going to be attracted to me with a bald head? I decided I'd better go ahead and take a wife now or face living as a hermit later."

That had to be one of the worst reasons to get married I've ever heard, although not as bad as another friend who decided to get married because he was tired of holding his gas.

I have another friend who began balding at an early age. He got himself a hairpiece which was quite expensive. He paid in the neighborhood of $500 for it. It did make him look much younger. He was aboard an Amtrak train one day and ventured down to the club car.

He had several cocktails and took himself a bit of a nap in his chair.

"When I awakened," he explained, "I felt for my wig and it was gone."

"I asked the bartender, 'Did you see anybody lift my toupee while I was asleep?'

"The bartender said, 'What color was it?'

"I said, 'Light brown.'

"The bartender said, 'That was your wig? I guess it fell off your head onto the floor. I thought it was some kind of hairy little animal that slipped onto the train and died. I swept it out when we stopped in Anniston.' "

There was once a horribly ugly, fat, baldheaded man who fell in love with a beautiful girl. He asked her out.
"I'd never go out with anybody like you," she said.

"You're ugly, fat and baldheaded and your clothes are a mess."

So the guy joins a fitness club and takes off seventy-five pounds. He gets himself a hair transplant and plastic surgery removes his ugliness. He goes to the best men's shop in town and buys himself a new wardrobe. He looks great.

He goes back to see the girl and asks her out again.

"Of course, I'll go out with you now," she said. "You're one of the most handsome men I've ever seen. Pick me up at eight."

Promptly at eight, the guy picks up the girl and they go strolling to his car.

"This is the happiest day of my life," he says.

Just at that moment, there is a flash of lightning. The man is hit and falls to the ground, where he is dying.

"Why me, Lord?" he asks. "Why did you have to do this to me now?"

God looks down and says, "That you, Sam? Sorry. I didn't recognize you."

One of the major changes I have noticed in my own body is that I now have a terrible case of the two-bellies.

I'm not certain what causes this (I once heard it explained that the chest arches had fallen), but I now have two very distinct bellies.

One starts just below the bottom of my rib cage and goes down to my navel, where there is an indentation. Below that indentation is where my second belly begins. It goes south from there.

I suppose I could diet or do some exercises like sit-ups to get back to having only one belly, but dieting and doing sit-ups are two things I wouldn't do for quadruple frequent flyer points.

The problem with the two-bellies is that once a man has them, he can forget about wearing blue jeans. Women, of course, love to see men in tight jeans. They have a fondness for the male buns, we learned at some point back in the seventies, and tight jeans are a marvelous way to show off your hindparts.

If I tried to put on a pair of tight jeans over my two bellies, I would be attempting the impossible, like attempting to put a hundred pounds of potatoes in a fifty-pound sack.

I once did go this far, however: I heard a radio commercial in which this guy was saying, "I can still play full-court basketball and can get dates with airheads, but my jeans don't fit like they used to.

"That's because a man's body changes as he gets older and to be comfortable in a pair of jeans, he needs a 'skoche' more room. So buy blah, blah, blah . . ."

That part about the "skoche" caught my interest. But, I asked myself, just how much is a "skoche"? I

consulted my dictionary, but I couldn't find "skoche."
I finally decided it was probably smaller than a cubit
and somewhat larger than a dab.

I went down to the jeans store.

A child of perhaps sixteen with orange hair came up
to me and introduced herself as a salesperson.

"I'd like a pair of jeans," I said.

"Like, I knew that, okay?" she responded. "I mean,
like, this is a jeans store, you know, and I didn't think
you were in here to buy, like, tires."

I considered calling over the manager, but then I saw
he also had orange hair and was maybe seventeen. I
simply decided to attempt to get through this as fast as
I could.

"I see your point, young woman," I said, smiling.
"But let us get on with our business. Do you have any
of those jeans with a 'skoche' more room?

"You mean the kind old men wear when they have
the two-bellies?" she asked.

"Something like that," I said.

"Sure, we got 'em. Follow me."

I followed her to the back of the store, where she
pulled out a box from under a table.

"Here they are," she said. "What size did you have
in mind?"

"I'd like to try thirty-four," I said.

"Don't waste my time, okay," said the salesgirl, pointing in the direction of my midsection.

"Well," I said, embarrassed now, "let me try thirty-six."

She brought out a pair of thirty-eights, sent me into the dressing room and said, "Don't get your skoche hung up when you try to zip these things up."

I put my regular pants back on and left the store. Now, I'm wearing pleated trousers with what the salesman, a distinguished gentleman with regular hair at the big and tall man shop, said had "a little extra give."

My hindparts are, for the most part, lost in such trousers, but the front covers both my bellies if I suck in. How long I can stay sucked in remains to be seen. I just hope I won't do anything foolish like marrying again simply because that would mean I could unsuck.

There are, however, certain advantages to growing a bit older and not having such things as the sexual energy (nor even the interest) as before. Somewhere, I read that males enter their sexual peak at age nineteen, while women reach theirs at thirty-five.

What this means is, remember all the times girls turned you away when you were younger and wanted to play around? When you're older, and they become the ones who are aflame with desire, while you merely smolder, you can get them back for what they did to you when you were a kid.

How delicious.

Throughout history, "Not tonight, dear, I have a headache" has been the cliché excuse for women to turn away men when they didn't want to have sex.

In my youth, I heard many other excuses, however. Listed below are a few of them:

—"I don't want to mess up my hair."

—"I'll never get my panty hose off in this little a space."

—"It's too early."

—"It's too late."

—"I've got a boyfriend in Korea. I just couldn't do this to him."

—"My cat's in the room."

—"I'm thinking of becoming a nun."

—"It's too cold."

—"It's too hot."

—"We'll wake up Margaret and Bob in the other room."

—And my favorite: "I'd like to have sex with you, but I'm afraid it would ruin what we have now."

There was even the story of the man who went to the doctor and was told he had only twelve hours to live.

He goes home and tells his young wife the news.

"What can I do to keep you happy these last twelve hours we are going to be together?" she asks.

"Let's make love," he says.

They make love for several hours.

"How much more time do you have, sweetheart?" his wife asks.

"Six more hours," he says.

"What can I do for you now?"

"Let's make love some more."

"I can't," says the wife.

"Why not?" the husband asks.

"Because," she answers. "I've got to get up in the morning and go to work. You don't."

Do women really understand how much pain and agony they cause a young man in his early, formative years when he is atop his sexual peak and would like to be atop many other things as well?

I think not. I was watching a movie recently entitled *All the Right Moves*. Tom Cruise is a teenager and he's parked in a dark place with his girlfriend. Tom Cruise is, as are most teenaged males, in excruciating heat.

His girlfriend allows him to drive her to a deserted spot. She allows him to begin kissing her. The next move he must make, as we all remember from our youth, is to get her in the prone position.

This isn't always an easy thing to accomplish, especially if you are in the front seat. I'm certain Jerry Falwell had something to do with it, although I can't prove it, but when bucket seats came out with the gearshift in the middle, it cut out front-seat fooling around almost completely.

Zelmer Higgens and Wyolene Turnipseed, a couple back in my hometown, were necking one night in Zelmer's GTO that had four-in-the-floor, two-barrel carburetors and flames on the sides.

He and Wyolene were attempting to take care of business in those bucket seats. At some point, Zelmer, in his passion, was attempting to put Wyolene is a strategic position and his arm knocked his GTO out of gear. The car started rolling down the hill. Zelmer tried to stop it, but Wyolene's bazoogas were in the way, and she had world-class bazoogas.

Finally, Zelmer's car came to a stop on the Atlanta and West Point R.R. tracks and around the corner came *The Crescent*, highballing it to Montgomery. Zelmer tried his best to crank the GTO, but he flooded it out. He and Wyolene had no choice but to abandon the car in order to save their lives.

Zelmer walked to the bottom of the hill below the tracks and turned his back on his car as he awaited the train coming to smash it.

"I just can't bear to watch, Wyolene," he said, as

Wyolene attempted to get all her clothing and parts back into a ladylike position.

The train came roaring by, but Zelmer heard no sound of crashing, bending metal. As he turned to see what had happened, Wyolene shouted, "Look out, Zelmer!"

But it was too late. The GTO had rolled off the tracks before the train arrived and was headed down the hill, straight for Zelmer.

He was in a body cast for nearly six weeks, his GTO was totaled and Wyolene left him for an older man who worked in a local cotton mill, and the entire sorry state of affairs was caused by bucket seats with the gearshift in the middle, which is why I brought up this story in the first place.

In the situation we were discussing before I went off on a tangent about Zelmer and Wyolene, Tom Cruise, meanwhile, doesn't have bucket seats in his car and manages to get his girlfriend down for what he hopes to be the count by simply planting a large kiss on her, while reaching behind her back with one arm and lifting from the back of her thighs with the other.

(This technique may be learned by anyone simply by watching professional wrestling. It is modeled after pro wrestling's "body slam.")

So now Tom Cruise has his girlfriend where he wants her. The kissing becomes even more passionate (tongues are being swapped and that sort of stuff) and

Tom begins to unzip and unfasten everything that now stands in his way.

No resistance yet from sweetie-pie.

Now, Tom Cruise is a loose cannon on the deck. He will not be denied. The camera shows his hands reaching for his ultimate prize, and he is allowed this with not so much as a squirm-to-struggle-free by his partner in all this.

You can feel the passion rising higher and higher and just when Tom Cruise is about to satisfy the begging, pleading, uncontrollable call of nature, his girlfriend cries, "No, no! This isn't right! You must stop now!"

Puh-leeze. This is cruel and unusual torment. This is what the horse they call the teaser must endure his entire career.

The evil temptress. She takes you to the brink of heaven, and then slams the door in your face.

Tom Cruise did what most men have done for centuries in his particular situation. He sat up in his seat, looked down at the evidence of his hungering state and tried to explain.

"I'm sorry I did this to you," he says. "I thought this time we had it made."

"Don't speak to me" is the reply he gets. There is nothing quite so uncomfortable to a man as a sulking member of the firm, or anyway you want to rearrange that phrase.

Tom Cruise's heart is beating, he is having to take deep gulps of breath, he is perspiring profusely, his hair is all down in his face, his clothes are wrinkled and his girlfriend says to him something like, "You rotten creep. How dare you make such an attempt on me!"

Tom reacts as most men do. He tries to apologize, which she, of course, will hear nothing of, and she demands to be taken home, and poor Teaser Tom is left an emotional, physical wreck.

"Why," all men who have been that sorry route should have asked their companions, "why did you (1) allow yourselves to be taken off in a car alone with someone obviously suffering from out-of-control glands, (2) allow the engine to be stopped, (3) graciously accept preliminary moves such as tongue-kissing and then participate actively in same, (4) allow yourself to be placed in a prone position, (5) not object at the unzipping and unbuttoning that ensued if you had absolutely no intention of fulfilling the desires of your partner that you helped build to their zenith?

"Huh? Why? Tell me."

But few of us rarely did that. We, like Tom Cruise, drove our girlfriend home and allowed them to tee up the ball on many, many future occasions, only to have them snatch it away Lucylike and send us up sprawling.

With the liberation of women, they have talked more openly and freely about sex, which is how a lot of those magazines like *Glamour* and *Cosmo* stay in business. Fashion and recipes are one thing, but when it became apparent how much women (after they pass the age where all that matters is tormenting boys) are interested in sex, they now feature such articles as:

"Favorite Sex Positions of the Rich and Famous."

"How to Lose Pounds and Have Great Sex, Too."

"How to Turn Your Lover into a Booger Under the Sheets."

At the same time, however, the male lovers being written about—older, wiser and interested in many more areas other than sex—were plotting how to get out of more sex and how to get even for the cold shower days of old.

"Sex does lose its place as the Number One priority for most men as they mature," said a man who had made his living as a salesman.

"When I was in my twenties and thirties, I'd come home from a sales trip and talk about the women I'd slept with," he went on. "In my forties and fifties, I'd talk about all the good food I ate. After that, I'd come home and remark how well my bowels had moved."

"It's funny," said another man, reacting to the same discussion. "I spent approximately the first forty years of my life trying to have sex with every woman I saw. After that, I've been trying to figure out ways to get out of it."

"It's not that I never want to have sex with my wife

anymore," said another interviewed for this chapter. "It's just that her timing is terrible."

"I'm right in the middle of watching *The Dirty Dozen* on cable and Telly Savalas is going crazy in the castle where all that German brass is.

"All of a sudden, my wife is right in my face trying to kiss me and get something started. If my wife had been involved in World War Two, we'd have probably lost it."

Women also seem to become sexually aroused the minute they see their lover embroiled in watching a sporting event on television.

It may be they must prove to themselves they are more desirable than a 3–2 change-up curve ball that nicks the corner of the plate.

We've all been through this:

"Honey, are you coming to bed now?" she says suggestively from the bedroom upstairs.

"Not just now, sweetheart. The Cubs have the bases loaded."

Thinking quickly, she goes to her closet and puts on a sexy night thing with all sorts of missing portions that she purchased at Frederick's of Hollywood. (Or LeRoy's of Dothan)—it's the same idea.)

"Does this," she asks her man, in a deep, sultry, inviting voice, "look more interesting to you than baseball?"

"You know, sweetheart, I've always said Sandberg is the best clutch hitter in baseball."

Desperate now, she removes the night thing and stands nude before her lover.

"Here I am, big boy," she says. "Take me."

". . . Out to the ball game," he is singing along with Harry Caray.

In other research I did for this book, I interviewed men, all over forty, and asked them how they were handling the fact that women, their wives or lovers (or both, I suppose), were expecting more sex than they really wanted to give out.

Said R.W. of Helena: "Whenever my wife starts demanding sex too often, I quit taking showers. You'd be surprised how long you can avoid having sex with your wife when you smell like a goat."

Explained D.B. of Oshkosh: "I try to explain to my woman about the ten o'clock rule. After ten o'clock, I'm just not interested anymore. At my age, doing anything more than sleeping or watching a rerun of *Barnaby Jones* after ten o'clock is totally out of the question."

Offered L.F. of Little Rock: "I really haven't had a problem with that in a long time. Back when I was in my late twenties, my wife cut me down to only twice a week. I figured I was pretty lucky, though. She cut two other fellers clean out."

There is another sad state of affairs, for men and women: when the male is struck with the dreaded inability to perform, especially when it is his intent to do exactly that.

The most traumatic point in a man's life comes when he is first unable to achieve an erection on demand. When the hand is no longer steady over a putt, when the eye can no longer pick up the spin on a curve ball, when the wind and the legs give way much quicker than before, it is terribly unsettling to a man. But when Oscar will not rise to the occasion, it is the end of the world.

There are many reasons men often aren't able to perform:

—Too much alcohol. At certain levels, alcohol can act as a sexual stimulant. Go past that level and your only hope is maybe there'll be an earthquake and she'll be out of the mood, too.

—Guilt: You know you're not supposed to be doing this. You're cheating, or she's too young, or you lied and told her you were once Johnny Wadd's stand-in. There obviously is a nerve that runs from your conscience to your business. Much of the time, you can ignore the messages the conscience transmits. Sometimes, however, that is impossible. Little voices begin speaking to you and you couldn't get anything moving with a flute.

—Fear. "Did you hear a car pull up?"

—Injury: It's basically impossible while lying in traction.

—Frustration: The harder you try, the softer it gets.

I'm sure there are other reasons having to do with diet, chemical disorders and the fact that your partner has a large mole with a hair sticking out of it on the front of her nose, but the ones listed above are the most common.

The question is, what can be done to achieve ultimate success in such a situation?

Of course, you could stop drinking, fooling around, and, thus, stop becoming guilty, as well as never trusting a woman who says, "My husband won't be home for hours."

Nobody is going to do any of those things, however, so here are a few more ideas:

—Excuse yourself, go into the bathroom and lecture it.

"How could you do something like this to me?" you might say. "I thought we were in this together. Now, let's go back in there and you behave."

—If this doesn't work, go back into the bathroom and try to shame it:

"Is this all the thanks I get?"

—If no success there, appeal to its intellect:

"Did you see her? I mean, she is the sort of thing that inspires sonnets. Surely, you aren't going to allow us to miss this opportunity?"

—Still no progress, so excuse yourself one more time and go back to the bathroom and climb out the window to avoid any further embarrassment.

How a male's partner reacts during such a crisis also has a lot to do with whether or not he eventually will achieve what he so desperately wants to achieve.

So as to avoid the male in question leaving a broken, defeated man, the partner should handle the situation, with great tenderness and understanding. Here are some things to say to make him feel better:

—"I know it's my fault."

—"Just be patient. We've got all night."

—"Why don't we stop, mix ourselves a drink, have a cigarette and just relax for a few minutes?"

—"Who do you like in the Lakers-Celtics game?"

Here are some things *not* to say:

—"So what everybody says about you is true, huh?"

—"Do you know this is the eighth time this has happened to me this week?"

—"Would you mind looking in the third drawer and handing me my vibrator?"

I do not want to laugh at impotency here. It is not a laughing matter. Happily, however, there are now ways to treat impotency, from counseling to drugs to implants, such as the one old man Hargrove over at the club had and is so proud of he always pumps it up before entering the shower.

(I was going to make up something about a new book that deals with the subject and say it is entitled *Stand Up for Impotency*. But I decided this was too serious a subject to do such a thing.)

There are a couple of more odds and ends I'd like to clear up here before moving on.

In an earlier chapter, I discussed The Chase and the fact that many men never lose their desire to take part in it. In this chapter, however, I have dealt with the curious fact that the male sexual energy and desire levels often decline as a man gets older. Is this, then, a contradiction on my part?

No. It's just that actually catching his prey becomes less important to a man after he reaches a certain age.

A philosopher once said, "After maturity, a man realizes that if he *could* have had sex with a woman, but, for one reason or the other didn't, it *still counts.*"

Taking a woman to bed remains a great boost to the male ego. But as a man ages, he can often become like those television fishermen. They get a great amount of enjoyment out of catching their fish, but after they have hooked them, they reel them into the boat and then throw them back into the water.

Continuing to play the game, but no longer having to get a hit each time at bat, takes a great deal of pressure off a man and allows him to live a much more relaxed life.

I also want to end on the optimistic note that a sexual relationship can continue to thrive and be fulfilling to both partners, regardless of age and the natural changes it brings, if certain tactics are followed.

We discussed earlier such couples as Cordie Mae and Hog Philpott and how they managed to keep their grapefruit squirting, but here are some more do's and don'ts in regard to achieving that end:

—*Do* keep an open mind. If your lover wants to fool around out in the backyard under a full moon, go ahead with it. Just be sure to take lots of bug spray, and if the next-door neighbors are having a cocktail party out back, don't make howling, baying or other passionate noises that would draw attention to yourselves.

If you are discovered anyway and are asked to join the party, accept graciously and *don't* call attention to your privates unless the hostess asks you to show her guests your cute tattoo.

—*Do* occasionally rent X-rated home video movies to keep up with the latest sexual tactics. *Don't,* however, try anything that involves a trapeze, a power tool, or a porcupine.

—*Do* attempt to maintain your lover's interest by occasionally wearing sexy apparel. *Don't* go to a K mart, a Home Depot, or L. L. Bean to do your shopping in this particular area.

—*Do* try positions other than the missionary. *Don't,* however, fail to be careful selecting other possible positions if one, or both, of you weigh more than three hundred pounds.

—*Do* play sensuous music during lovemaking. If Boxcar Willie and Slim Whitman are your ideas of sensuous music, *don't* tell anybody.

—*Do* listen if your lover wants to discuss the possibility of engaging in group sex. If your lover is a member of a motorcycle gang, the National Rifle Association, the Rotary Club, or Daughters of the Boxer Rebellion, don't agree to anything until you've talked it over with your lawyer or chiropractor.

—*Do* discuss with friends your sexual problems, ideas or innovations. *Don't* get involved in swinging with any couples named Big Al and Lotsa Mama, Mad Dog and Wild Thing or Jim and Tammy Faye.

—*Do* wear exciting perfumes or colognes to keep your lover interested. If your lover gets turned on by the scent of kerosene, *don't* miss a payment on the fire insurance for your house, or own a dalmatian.

CHAPTER NINE

T he last thing I remember about condoms before, say, a couple of years ago, was the time Alvin Bates, the class nerd, brought one to chemistry class as part of a project to explain expanding gases.

Alvin got up in front of the class, not to mention Mr. Scoggins, the teacher, and dropped a couple of Alka-Seltzers into a shot glass. He then put a condom over the shot glass and whatever it is that bubbles out of Alka-Seltzer made the condom stick straight up.

The boys in the class laughed. The girls, with the exception of Adella Lemaster, who was very religious and ran screaming out of the class, all giggled. Mr. Scoggins cleared his throat several times and quickly told Alvin to cease his demonstration and sit down.

As it turned out, Alvin had no idea what he had done. As he was going through his father's sock drawer one day, looking for a black, over-the-calf pair to wear with his sandals and Bermuda shorts to a Sunday school picnic, Alvin came upon several coin-sized packages.

Always the inquisitive type and always eager for knowledge (Alvin subscribed to *Grit, Boys Life,* and *Popular Science,* and never missed *Mr. Wizard* on television), he opened one of the packages and discovered a curious balloonlike instrument.

He asked his father, who was the county agent for the Farm and Home Extension Service, to identify what he had found in the sock drawer.

Alvin's dad, Mr. Bates, told him it was a sheath used to keep carrots from getting hurt from sudden frosts. As Alvin planned his chemistry demonstration, he thought those carrot covers would be just the thing for his expanding gases trick and took one from his dad's sock drawer.

I didn't mention Alvin in the chapter regarding people who've never had sex, because I'm just not certain in his case. After college at Clemson, Alvin joined the Peace Corps and last I heard of him, he had been taken prisoner by some left wing group attempting a coup in one of those countries that looks like an eye test when you spell it out.

Alvin was busy on a project to convince the natives

to stop wearing loincloths and wear knee-length woolen shorts that had been donated by postal workers instead, when he was taken away by rebels.

In a terse statement in late 1969, the State Department denied there ever being an Alvin Bates in the Peace Corps.

Even if the rebels didn't execute him and released him back to the natives, I figure they probably hung him, or worse, for convincing them to take off their comfortable loincloths for those scratchy woolen shorts.

In either case, it's doubtful Alvin ever did know the particular joy of sex, but one can never be too sure when loincloths are involved. If I hear from Alvin and can clear this matter up before I finish this book, I will pass on any answer I might get for our question.

Anyway, after Alvin used the condom in chemistry class. I didn't hear much about condoms anymore until recently when the AIDS scare came along.

That's because condoms (a.k.a. prophylactics, a.k.a. rubbers—and those are the only other names I ever knew them by) were virtually replaced by other means of birth control such as the pill, contraceptive foam, and the IUD which, incidentally, is DUI spelled backwards.

We must also remember that every condom machine in every truck stop displayed the notice, "This product should be used for the prevention of disease only."

This, I presume, was so that if anybody used a condom and it leaked and somebody got pregnant anyway, they couldn't sue the condom company. There's no telling how much some lawyer charged condom companies for thinking of that.

There was, of course, a concern for getting venereal disease back then. Went the wisdom of the day, "Better not catch the clap because you're going to have a helluva time convincing your wife she's got to have a shot for *your* kidney infection."

But I remain certain that not one in a thousand condoms were used because of a fear of getting a disease. They were used because it was hell to pay if you got a girl pregnant in those days.

The girl's mother would send her off to a home and, if you lived in a small town, they'd talk about you for eons and the preacher would include you in his annual antifornication sermon, which, at home, always came just before the Fourth of July Street Dance when the tempting moan of the steel guitar, mixed with the warm night air and six bottles of Calgary Malt Liquor, could fling a craving for the flesh on the saved and unsaved alike.

Having said that, however, let me also say there were only a couple of girls I knew of who got pregnant out of wedlock when I lived back home, and we're talking eighteen years here, which is to say either there was a lot of condom use going on or there wasn't much serious woo being pitched.

Quite frankly, I go for the latter explanation. As I have said earlier, the sexual revolution was a ways off then, and in the immortal words of my boyhood friend and idol, Weyman C. Wannamaker, Jr., a great American, after thirty-four successive dates that didn't come across, "If I ever scored in this town, I'd take out an ad and announce it in the county paper."

Still, once we reached our teens, we felt to walk around without a condom in our wallets would be to ignore completely all the advantages of preparedness. God, what if lightning struck and there you were without, as we said back then, *protection*? (Later, this term became a byword of a number of feminine hygiene products' advertising campaigns, but let's don't get into that.)

There were a number of ways to come into possession of your first condom. You could take the easy route by finding out where your father kept his, or you could show your manhood by actually buying one for yourself.

There were even two ways of doing that. The easiest way was to go to a service station or truck stop and go into the men's room where the condom machines were located.

And what wondrous machines those were! Usually, there were several selections of condoms, as there are several selections in a gum or cigarette machine, not to mention other sexually related products, such as a cream called "Dee-Lay" to avoid premature getting through, and a tiny book of sex jokes everybody had already heard.

As far as their condoms were concerned, there was one that came in "exciting, exotic colors," another that featured a "nipple end," and then there was the celebrated "French Tickler," to be purchased at risk because of its ability to "drive her wild!"

There were certain procedures to follow when purchasing one's first condom in a restroom. First, you had to remember to bring quarters. To go to the cashier and ask for change and then to go directly into the restroom certainly would expose your intent.

Not only would that be embarrassing, but it also could get back to your mother.

The other thing to remember was, once you were safely inside the restroom, to lock the door. Then, it was absolutely necessary to slide the coin holder into the machine very quietly so nobody outside could hear and, again, know of your evil scheme.

There also was a time element involved here. One had to be mindful of just how long the exercise of buying a condom took. You had to stay in the bathroom long enough to, well, go to the bathroom, because if you came out quickly everybody would know. "Look at that kid," they'd say. "He didn't stay in the bathroom very long, so we know he was in there buying rubbers."

Of course, if you took too long, then there must have

been something else you were doing in the bathroom other than using the facility, and what else could that be other than you were buying condoms?

The ultimate in obtaining a condom was, however, actually going into a drugstore and buying one across the counter from a pharmacist.

This took some guts, even if you lived in a large town and went to a drugstore where there was absolutely no chance of anybody you knew seeing you in this act.

Lee Marvin would have had a difficult time convincing *The Dirty Dozen* to attempt to pull off such a thing in a small town, however, where anybody from your Aunt Hattie to your typing teacher could catch you.

To be quite frank, I never got up the courage to buy a condom in a drugstore until I was in my middle thirties. I'm not certain why, but buying condoms in public always seemed to be letting a lot of other people in on the fact that you were having sex with somebody. You know the pharmacist is grinning inside, and will talk about you when you leave.

The other bad thing that could happen in this scenario is the machine could be broken or out of condoms and you would not only be denied the object of all your effort, but you'd lose your quarter, too.

You couldn't bang on the machine like you would a soft drink box that took your money because that would make a lot of noise. You couldn't go complain to the owner, either, because he would say something like, "Son, you're too young to be buying something like that."

In fact, I learned later in life that some service station and truck stop owners had condom machines installed in their restrooms but never had them filled.

"We even had one in the ladies' restroom where I worked," a man told me. "There never was anything in them, though, because no woman was going to complain that the rubber machine was out at a truck stop. No telling how much money the guy I worked for made with that scam."

Some guys had enough guts and bravura to pull it off when I was a kid though, and they were admired and spoken of in hushed, reverent tones.

Legend even had it that one twelve-year-old walked up to the pharmacist in Leebold's Drug Store and said, "I want a condom."

The pharmacist replied, "Son, are you sure that's what you want?"

"Yes sir," said the kid. "I want one of those French Ticklers, too."

"But don't you know what that will do to a woman, young man?" the pharmacist continued.

"No," said the kid, "but it'll make a goat jump six inches off the ground."

I know one more like that.

A young man meets a girl. They have a few dates and at the young man's pleading, the girl agrees to have sex with him the following Saturday night at the drive-in theater. This is a modern-day story.

She insists, however, he bring protection—that word again—so he goes down to the drugstore and walks back to the pharmacist and says, "I'll have a condom."

The pharmacist winks and says, "Hot date, huh?"

"Can't miss," says the young man. "This girl is the hottest."

He walks to the door at the girl's home the following Saturday and she says, "Come in for a minute and meet my parents."

The young man meets the parents and then says to his date, "Honey, we can go to the drive-in anytime. Why don't we stay here and play Monopoly with your parents?"

The girl is quite befuddled, but the young man is insistent.

Around midnight, the young man yawns and indicates he must leave. The girl follows him to his car. She is angry.

"I didn't know," she says, "that you were such a fan of Monopoly."

"And I didn't know," he replies, "that your father was a pharmacist."

Condoms are more than back now. They are the rage of the sexual age because of AIDS. No matter your sexual preference, we are told, use a condom or you could die.

Whereas condoms were once talked about in hushed tones and brought on giggles and blushing, they're advertised on billboards today, yea, even on television.

Companies that manufacture condoms say their sales are skyrocketing and there's even something called National Condom Week, with festivities all over the country that include college students throwing condoms filled with water at one another, *condom sculpting*, and, believe it or not, a game called pin-the-condom-on-the-man.

We might even see Alvin Bates, presuming he's still alive, as part of National Condom Week, doing his expanding gases demonstration or blowing condoms up and making them into shapes of bunny rabbits and dachshunds.

I, of course, am for anything that will halt the number of people dying from AIDS, but there are certain things about condoms that will keep some people from using them, and I am speaking only of heterosexuals here. I hope I am not homophobic and I really don't care if somebody wants to do it with a Ford Escort, but please have the decency to rent a motel room.

The major problem with a condom is that it's not

that easy to install one of those things, especially in the dark.

Condom manufacturers apparently don't realize this and make no effort to facilitate the process. They put condoms in all sorts of containers, such as little plastic boxes which are supposed to be easy to open, but aren't.

Here you are in a glorious moment of passion, and you have to call time-out. And let's say all that was was happening between you and your partner just sort of came about without any preplanning.

The worst thing would be if you didn't have any condoms on hand. You'd have to get up, get dressed, and go down to the drugstore. And what if it were late at night?

Drugstores do have those numbers on the front to call in case of an emergency, but I don't think you could get a druggist to come down and open his store at two A.M. just so you could finish what had been started.

And even if you've got condoms, you've still got to get up, turn on the light and look for them. Of course, they are not in the drawer where you put them and you have to look for fifteen minutes before you finally find them behind the Lavoris in the medicine cabinet.

By that time, a lot of things could have happened. One, if this is your debut with this partner, he or she could be having second thoughts by this time.

"Listen, Lester," she could say, "it really would have been great, but I'll have to take a rain check. I've got a meeting in the morning and this thing has just sort of dragged on. . . ."

If you are a young man, this sort of delay probably wouldn't be all that critical. However, older men do have the occasional problem of losing their edge, and there's nothing that will lose it any quicker than having to run all over the house looking for a condom, stubbing your toe on the furniture in the process.

There is also the negative aspect of condom use that has to do with some of the male's sexual pleasure being taken away by the use of such a device.

"It's sort of like taking a shower in a raincoat" is how it was once described.

Still, having condoms back after all these years has been interesting, and has provided the opportunity to look back on my youth and my first days of sexual awareness.

There is, of course, the controversy today over whether or not teenage students should be aware of condoms, not only as a protection against disease, but as a means of controlling teen pregnancies.

There should not be a controversy here because kids already know everything there is to know these days soon after their potty training is over. And, as far as I'm concerned, anything that would stop the birthing of unwanted babies is a great idea.

I mentioned in an earlier chapter about the stink that occurred in a Carroll County (Georgia) school when a health instructor used a cucumber to show students how a condom should be used.

Parents were up in arms, and I suppose a cucumber is a bit too graphic. What we need, then, is a universally accepted phallic symbol that can be used to show young people how to put on a condom.

Bananas are out, of course. Also flashlights, beer cans, and Polish sausages.

I think the sweet potato is the answer to all this. There is absolutely nothing suggestive about a sweet potato, unless one remembers the 1800s drinking song entitled, "Don't Bend Over in the Garden, Granny, You Know Them Taters Got Eyes."

Now that all that is settled, we can leave condoms with one final condom story:

Mr. and Mrs. Wojohowitz, Ira and Hazel were in their eighties. Mr. Wojohowitz had retired after a successful career as a banker.

Their children were all grown and doing well. One evening, as the Wojohowitzes were watching television, Hazel says to Ira:

"You know, my dear, I've been thinking that we should get out more. All we're doing here is just sitting around waiting to die."

"Where would you like to go, my dear?" asks Mr. W.

"Somewhere romantic. I've got it! Let's go on a week-

long cruise. It will be like old times. We can even make love as we did when we were younger."

Mr. Wojohowitz gets up out of his chair, puts on his hat and coat and walks down to the corner drugstore where he has shopped for years.

He says to the pharmacist, "I'd like to have two bottles of seasick pills and four condoms."

The pharmacist fills the order and Mr. Wojohowitz returns home where Hazel, meanwhile, has been thinking again.

"Ira, darling," she begins. "Why should we be on a cruise for only a week? What else do we have to do? Why don't we go on a month-long cruise? Think of how much romance we could have in a month's time."

Back to the drugstore goes Mr. Wojohowitz.

"I'd like twelve bottles of seasick pills," he says to the pharmacist, "and twenty condoms."

Back home again, Hazel says:

"Why should we be gone for just a month? Who'll miss us? Let's go on a year-long cruise. Let's go around the world and make love like we used to."

Back to the drugstore.

"I'd like fifty bottles of seasick pills," says Mr. Wojohowitz to the druggist, "and a hundred forty condoms."

The pharmacist, intrigued by all this, finally says, "I don't want to be personal, Mr. Wojohowitz, but if it makes you that sick, why do you do it so often?"

CHAPTER TEN

A

few closing notes:

At some point in this book, I had to deal with the fact
that a great many of today's rock singers are using
dirty lyrics and keeping Tipper Gore, who came in
about eighteenth as the nation's new first lady, up at
night.

You will recall that Mrs. Gore, Sen. Al's wife, spoke
out about all of this and wanted, among other things,
lyrics of rock songs printed on the outside of albums
and cassettes so parents could read what their children
are listening to.

I am, of course, aware of such people as George Michael and Prince (I'm not certain if that's his first name or his last), and AC/DC and their songs with sexual overtones, as well as I am aware of the upcoming group, Stark Nekkid and the Car Thieves with their new chartbuster, "Let Me Kiss You Square on Your Woo-Woo."

However, I must say that dirty lyrics are nothing new. My father even taught me songs with dirty lyrics when I was a child. My favorite was:

> There's a soldier in the grass
> With a bullet up his (bad word),
> Get it out, get it out,
> Like a good Girl Scout.

Later, in the second grade, I learned this one:

> There's a place in France
> Where the women wear no pants
> And the men go 'round
> With their yo-yo's hanging down.

As a teenager growing up in the South, I soon heard about a group called Doug Clark and the Hot Nuts. They performed on many southern campuses and word leaked down to the high schools of some of their lyrics.

One song began:

> Roly-poly, tickle my holey . . .

Then, there was the signature:

> Nuts, hot nuts,
> Get 'em from the peanut man,
> Hey, nuts, hot nuts
> Get 'em any way you can
> See that girl, dressed in green
> She ain't nothin' but a (bad word) machine,
> Nuts, hot nuts
> Get 'em from the peanut man.

The song that captured a generation whose parents wouldn't let them go see such movies as *Bad Seed, A Summer Place* and *The Gene Krupa Story*, however, was the legendary "Louie, Louie" by the Kingsmen.

The lyrics to "Louie, Louie" were barely discernible, so it was natural to assume they were dirty.

From everywhere came students who claimed to have a copy of just what the "Louie, Louie" lyrics really were. I saw at least five hundred different versions in my own high school alone.

It was also rumored you could get a 45 record of "Louie, Louie" down to 33 and hear all the dirty words.

It sounded like the same song, only performed by people with their mouths full of Penzoil.

School officials soon got wind of all this, of course, and banned the song from being played at any school function such as the Key Club dance or the "El Cid" celebration, held annually by the Spanish Club.

At this point, I intended to put in the real lyrics to "Louie, Louie," but the owner of the song refused to allow me to do so, even after I offered him money and two tickets to a Conway Twitty concert.

So, what I decided to do was to make up my own lyrics and at the same time inject some much-needed romance into bowling with a sensitive ballad about a young man in a classic romantic crisis one night at Louie's Bowl-A-Rama.

> "Louie, Louie, Oh Baby, We Gotta Bowl"
> (sung to the tune of "Louie, Louie")
> > *Chorus:*
> > Louie, Louie, oh baby,
> > We gotta bowl
> > A fine little girl is waiting for me
> > I cruise on down in my Caddy
> > We meet to bowl at Louie's Lanes
> > It's good as sex, and no migraines.
> >
> > Louie, Louie, oh baby,
> > We gotta bowl.

Three nights and days I tell my friends
I love that girl, she hits the pins
She don't sweat much and buys the beer
All my friends can't help but leer.

Louie, Louie, oh baby,
We gotta bowl.

I stick my fingers in the bowling ball
And then I see my downfall
A cocktail waitress, her tight dress slit
I'm 7-10 babe, I've gotta split.

Louie Louie, oh baby,
I gotta bowl.

In my research, I did manage to obtain the lyrics of many of today's popular songs, and, I must admit, they are quite graphic. The main difference I noticed between the sexy songs of my generation and the sexy songs of today was ours were for the fun of it. The filthy-mouthed warblers of today seem mad at somebody.

Vinnie Vincent's charming "I Wanna Be Your Victim" talks about how he wants to be penetrated, dominated and incinerated by the love of his life. My favorite image is the one where he lovingly describes how his girlfriend makes him scream and cream in his sleep.

I wanted to be able to print the lyrics here, for your reading pleasure, but I guess Vinnie has some taste, after all, because:

PERMISSION TO USE LYRICS DENIED

Then, there is the romantic "Eat Me Alive" by Judas Priest:

> Gut-wrenching frenzy
> That deranges every joint
> I'm going to force you at gunpoint
> To eat me alive.

And all Elvis ever sang was "Hunka, hunka burnin' love."

There are two things I would like to point out to Tipper Gore here. Yes, such lyrics as the above are angry, hostile, and full of violence, but the artists have at least had the good taste to sing along with such loud, screeching, cacophonous accompaniment that it is almost impossible to pick up the lyrics simply by listening to a record or tape.

If we demand lyrics be printed on the front of albums or cassette then we are giving children an opportunity to find out exactly what it is Judas Priest is saying.

Now, they probably think it's just some guy screaming into a microphone with a train wreck going on behind him.

Point two, Mrs. Gore, is that you are from Tennessee, which is the home of country music. Have you listened to country music lately?

I have been a country fan for many years, as are many adults, but country's lyrics leave very little to the imagination and they are quite discernible.

I frankly don't know what got into Conway Twitty. I'm as big a Conway Twitty fan as the next forty-two-year-old with a truck stop jukebox in his background, but I don't know if Conway is setting a good example when he sings, "Even with your hair up in curlers/I'd still love to lay you down."

Or, "There's a tiger in these tight-fittin' jeans." Also, it was Conway who cut the country version of the Pointer Sisters' "Slow Hand," a song about premature ejaculation, and it was Conway who sang "Don't call him a cowboy if you ain't seen him ride," with such lyrics as, "If he's not good in the saddle, you won't be satisfied."

I don't know what to make of all of this, but I would, had I the opportunity, like to point out to today's rock singers that, in my humble opinion, sex is a lot more fun when nobody gets hurt. I'd also like to point out to Conway Twitty that he's too old to be singing about all that stuff and he is making it difficult on the husbands of the forty-plus wives that listen to his music. They warm up to such lyrics and then expect their aging veterans to put out the fire.

I'd also like to know what's kept Dick Clark looking so young all these years, but I'm afraid to ask.

SIGN ON A CHURCH MARQUEE: "Tired of sin? Come on in." Underneath was scrawled, "If not, call Shirley, 555-3132."

Sexual myths of the 1950s:

1. If you put cigarette ashes into a girl's Coke, she will become a wanton seductress.

2. You can become pregnant if you are French kissing and swallow some of the boy's saliva.

3. If, when you are holding a girl's hand she begins to rub her finger on your palm, it means she wants to do it.

4. All airline stewardesses are beautiful and highly sexed.

5. Rock Hudson is gay.

The only one of the previous that turned out to be true: 5.

Jimmy Swaggart and Jim Bakker die and go to heaven. They are met by St. Peter.

"Frankly, guys," says St. Peter, "both of you are a little suspect, but I tell you what I'm going to do.

"I going to let you in and give you both a set of wings, but you're going to be on probation. At any time during the next ten years if you even think of anything bad, your wings are going to fall off. Here's a Bible for each of you to carry to remind yourself of what I have said."

Several years later, Swaggart and Bakker are walking along and they see a gorgeous blond angel walk past. It is more than Swaggart can stand.

"I've got to have a dirty thought," he bellowed, and tossed his Bible to the ground. Then, he thought better.

"I just can't do it," he said, and bent over in front of Bakker to pick up his Bible, at which time Bakker's wings fell right off.

I know who first said, "Making love to your wife is like striking out the pitcher," but I'm sworn to secrecy.

A piece of graffiti I saw in a men's room once I never quite understood and it probably doesn't have anything to do with sex, but it might:

Time flies like an arrow.
Fruit flies like a banana.

Hear about the Scotsman who had to give up sex
and golf at the same time? He tore his condom and
lost his ball.

Did Brigham Young ever have to pay any alimony?

Another nice, fairly clean sex joke:

A man goes to see his doctor, complaining of horrible
headaches. The doctor prescribes this medicine and
then that medicine. Nothing works.

Finally the doctor says to his patient, "I can't think
of anything else to do for you. The only thing I might
suggest is you try what I do when I have a headache."

"And what is that?" asked the patient.

"Whenever I have a headache," the doctor explained,
"I put my head between my wife's breasts and leave it
for an hour and my headache goes away. I don't know
if it will work for you, but it's worth a try."

Six weeks later, the man returns to his doctor and
says, "Great news! Your headache remedy worked!"

"Great," said the doctor.

"Yeah," the patient went on. "I did exactly what
you told me to do and I haven't had a headache since.

And one other thing, doc. You've got a great-looking house."

Nobody really went to school with a girl named Fonda Peters, but did you ever notice how many guys say they did?

A few of my favorite dirty limericks, and I have no idea who authored any of them:

> There was a young lady from Nizes
> Who had breasts of two different sizes
> One was small, and round like a ball,
> And the other was large, and won prizes.
>
> There was a young lady from Norway
> Who stood on her head in the doorway
> She said to her man,
> Get off the divan,
> I think I've discovered one more way.
>
> There was a young man named Skinner
> Who took a young lady to dinner.
> So he wouldn't be late,
> He picked her up before eight,
> And by quarter to ten it was in her.

Dinner, not Skinner.

Skinner was in her before dinner.

Prince Charles, while visiting the United States in 1977, attended a University of Georgia football game. Trying to be friendly and do what they could for Anglo-American relations, a Georgia fraternity unveiled a huge sign as the Prince walked onto the field at Sanford Stadium that read, "The Prince Does It Dawg Style."

Enough of this nonsense. As I pointed out in the beginning of this book, I'm not dedicating it to anybody. If I were, though, I'd probably dedicate it to the guy who came home late one night and his wife said, "You've been out with those sorry friends of yours again, have you?"

He said that he had.

"And how much money did you spend?" she asked, accusingly.

"A hundred and forty," he answered.

"A hundred and forty!" bellowed his wife. "You spent that in just one night. Do you know how long it would take me to spend that much money?"

"Let's see," said the husband. "You don't drink, right?"

"Right." 244

"And you don't gamble, right?"

"Right."

"And you've got your own (bad word) too. Right?"

"Right."

"Well," the guy said to his wife, "I figure right at a lifetime."

ABOUT THE AUTHOR

Lewis Grizzard is a man dedicated to making America laugh. His syndicated column now reaches 300 newspapers around the world, and several chiropractors' offices. When he's not writing or making speeches, he's recording comedy albums and playing golf. His golf game has many comedic qualities, with the exception of the cheating.

Lewis lives in Atlanta with a demented black labrador retriever named Catfish, who doesn't seem to think that Lewis is all that funny. But he does enjoy, on occasion, chewing on one of Lewis's previous nine books.